PRACTICAL SPIRITUALITY

How to Use Spiritual Power to Create Tangible Results

James Arthur Ray

SunArk Press
Carlsbad, California
JamesRay.com

ISBN: 0-9667400-3-3

Layout by Orange Pineapple Productions, LLC.

SunArk Press
Carlsbad, California
Printed in the U.S.A.

Third Edition

Table of Contents

Introduction

EVERY great teacher, saint, and sage since time immemorial has told us power is not something you can obtain outside yourself. True power is not something you wield over people or circumstances: Authentic power is an awareness and level of consciousness that transcends yet includes the physical plane. In other words, regardless of the situations or circumstances that may confront you, true power remains unmoved. You cannot control the waves, but you can learn to surf.

The path of power is a warrior's path... and it will never be crowded.

While possessing and increasing power is the outcome of every human being on the planet (whether the individual is consciously aware of it or not), few reach their potential. Most have been conditioned to believe that power comes from outside results or circumstances instead of from personal expansion of consciousness. Truly enlightened sages are masters of their own universe, and they recognize that every time consciousness is raised, the externals of life change accordingly.

The great paradox is that once money, material goods, or any external are no longer your point of focus, you will tend to have more of them. However, a greater paradox still is that the more power you wield, and therefore the more "things" you *can* have, the greater your tendency to care less about them. Higher levels of power and consciousness invariably shift priorities.

Since childhood I have had an unquenchable thirst for truth, rarely finding satisfaction in the traditional answers. For more than two decades I have worked with many teachers and traveled great distances to consciously reconnect with who I am. The processes that escalate consciousness are timeless and universal. While accessing power may be simple, it is not easy, nor is it supposed to be. Whether you study Jesus, Buddha, Krishna, or any other sage, you will find their lives filled with discipline, rites of passage, and struggle between their divine and human selves.

The romantics will tell you that we must "return to Eden" or "awaken to our original state of divinity." I consider this childish. First of all, Eden is an allegory or illustration of the human journey from ignorance to independence and not to be taken literally. Consciousness and Spirit are always for fuller expression and expansion: always moving forward, never moving back. A return to Eden is a return to unconscious incompetence, a return to ignorance.

From Eastern thought we learn, "As is the macrocosm so the microcosm; as is the cosmic mind so is the human mind." In the West, this thought was also expressed by Hermes Trismegistus: "As above, so below." Evolution and the escalation of power at greater degrees are the reason every living entity enters the physical plane. Whether it's the butterfly bursting the cocoon, the flower breaking through the soil, a baby being born, or a level of consciousness being obtained, you will find the same battle: the death of one level of existence becoming the birth of a new level. For anything new to live, something first must die. Birth and death are partners in the eternal dance.

Evolution is a battle and also a birthing process.

This struggle of death and rebirth has always been present in evolution and always will be. The omission of this journey in Jesus' life by traditional religion has caused him to seem inaccessible to "mere mortals," although this was neither his intention nor his teaching. As a result, we have developed a religious belief *about* Jesus rather than *of* the Christ. Likewise, there are many beliefs *about* Siddhartha rather than *of* the Buddha.

Over the years, we have come to treat Christ or Buddha as the actual name of the individual, rather than the level of consciousness they obtained. A study of history proves there were many Christs, virgin births, miracles, and resurrections years before the followers of Jesus claim they occurred. Truth is timeless.

The true person of power is the individual whose objective is to step into full Christ or Buddha consciousness. And while this is the birthright and ultimate destiny of every individual on the planet, the number of people who are pursuing it is small. Stop people on the street and ask them to define their ultimate life goal, and how many would answer "enlightenment"? Few to none.

My personal experience from the teachers who have tutored me, the books I have read, the realities I have explored, and the traditions I have studied prove that nothing happens by accident. Everything is orchestrated in perfect order and in perfect timing, whether the ego or small self grasps this concept or not.

As a result, you even have this book for a reason: You have it because you are supposed to. There is a purpose for you in reading this page at this time in your life and at this time in history. There are no accidents, and you are most probably already on the path. Choosing the path is a unique and commendable event. Staying on the path is rare indeed.

Many of the concepts presented here will already be known to you at some level, so the purpose of your reading will be to re-mind you (in other words, to put you in mind of them again). Some may seem more profound than others, some more mystical, some more practical, yet be assured they are all necessary and they will appeal to you based upon where you are at this point in your own personal journey of power.

This book contains twenty-nine principles to realize your infinite self. Many will seem simple to comprehend intellectually yet challenging to implement practically. There may even be some insights and angles you are exposed to in a new way or for the first time.

Nevertheless, you are destined to know this work. Possibly, now is your time to walk the path of the warrior... the path of power. As you read the word *warrior*, it may conjure images of a violent, testosterone-filled male. This is not the warrior spoken of or needed. The warrior spirit is male *and* female. The warrior I refer to does not engage in battle with external issues or individuals. The warrior of true power does battle within the internal realms of consciousness, in the battle to be unique, to break away from the programming of the collective masses and to stroll the halls of the gods.

Rest assured that the true battle in your life has nothing to do with your environment, your job, the economy, or anything outside of you. The greatest battle lies within you and is with a most formidable opponent.

Those who pursue their divinity may be perceived as misfits, mavericks, and outsiders (MMOs) by the collective consciousness, but that is okay and exactly as it should be. Be forewarned that this warrior battle is not for the faint of heart. There will be few who understand you, and even fewer will follow... for a time.

There is a movement of power beginning to build in our world. The existing ways of thinking have run their course, and a new breed of spiritual warriors are pursuing and practicing timeless truths in a modern way. Consciousness evolves and expands (moves forward); it doesn't contract ever! Our call is not to return to traditional values or ancient teachings and practices. Our call is to tap that which is timeless and apply it in today's world.

Instead of returning to the good old times, we are called to cultivate a "modern timelessness," to find what is enduring and apply it today. I invite you to join me and a growing group of MMOS to bring in a new way of living–a new level of consciousness and power unlike anything our world has ever experienced.

We stand poised and ready as a planet. This is not a foo-foo fluffy, New Age notion that, despite good intentions, in many ways has become a new iteration of the very system it desired to change. Too many well-meaning seekers have rubbed their crystals, stepped into the light, explored past lives, and consulted their psychics. While these practices may have a time and a place, they have most often created sofa warriors instead of initiates of true power. No achievement of great importance will magically arrive in your life without developing commitment and will.

The warrior's path of power is a mystical and practical advancement of the individual and collective consciousness. Mystical practice is an empty vessel without discipline and practical application. Power is an empty vessel unless it produces tangible results.

Welcome to the path of power!

PRACTICAL SPIRITUALITY

Transcend the Ego

WE start here because transcending your ego will definitely be the single most difficult challenge you will ever face. The ego is your proverbial blessing and curse. The ego blessing comes in the form of an individual identity, which must be developed for the advancement of your consciousness. This identity is the factor separating you from the masses and allowing you to stand unique. While this separation or uniqueness is ultimately an illusion, it is a necessary step in your advancement. Normally, the individual ego identity begins to develop and separate from the rest of the world between three and six years of age. Psychologists call this "individuation."

While developing this uniqueness is a necessary checkpoint in the evolution of consciousness, it must not become a campground. Unfortunately, most people drive tent pegs here, building their life-long residence.

Ultimately, we all come from one source. Call that source God, Energy, Spirit, or whatever name is to your liking, but every great teacher, from scientist to sage, has communicated that this source is the basic building block of every physical entity in existence. Your ego is nothing more than a bundle of imagination and memory–it is *not* you. You are an energy field, and as an aspirant of power, you must see yourself this way.

Recent discoveries in the tropical rainforest suggest that all the "different" trees are actually operating from the same universal root system: many manifestations of one infinite source, many individual energy fields operating in a larger collective field.

Likewise, you are a unique manifestation of the one eternal and infinite self. However, the ego thinks itself separate and independent and, while this is necessary early in your journey, this line of thinking is childish and limiting as evolution unfolds.

The ego is an insecure and wily character with an insatiable appetite. Its primary motivation is self-importance—more, better, bigger, best. Your ego is most often the primary drain on energy and power that you possess. Think about this: How much energy do you burn on a daily basis defending yourself? Protecting and projecting the correct self-image? Attempting to win people over? To have them like and approve of you? Convincing others that you are the best—or the worst? That you are worthy or unworthy? That you are the most loved, the most despised, the most mistreated, unfortunate, blessed—the list is endless! The ego's number-one fear is extinction or death; therefore, it sucks your energy like a vampire, attempting in every way imaginable to make itself real.

All great traditions teach that this death of the ego must happen in the pursuit of power. Furthermore, great advances of consciousness are almost always preceded by a "fall" or difficult life situation.

Only when you tame this governor of true power can you ever hope to actualize your potential.

Like a wild boar on steroids, the ego will never be satisfied, because it is focused on externals. Satisfaction, joy, peace, and true power are internal. While you intellectually may agree with this, owning this concept is a different matter.

The ego hates change and unpredictability, wanting to be comfortable and to follow a routine—that's how it maintains an illusion of control. To take back your true power you must constantly be awake and alert.

One of the ways to tame the ego is to take it off guard. You must become comfortable with discomfort. Break your routine; do things that keep you sharp. Do things that your current self-image could never imagine you doing. In my JOURNEY OF POWER® curriculum, I am constantly providing participants with the opportunity to shatter their self-image and step outside the comfortable. To advance, you must do the same.

The moment you challenge yourself to do something you could never dream of doing—to push the envelope, whether physically, mentally, or spiritually—you have expanded your possibilities and power.

For three years I disciplined myself to get up at 4 AM every single day to exercise and meditate, no matter what time I went to bed and no matter how I felt. This is the last thing my whiny ego wanted to do on the nights when I had only three hours of sleep! The best time to prove you are a warrior and truly in charge is when your ego chatter tells you *not* to do something that is uncomfortable. Do it anyway!

After three years this practice became comfortable and routine, so it was time to change again. This time I chose to sleep until I awakened on my own—no matter what time it was. If I awakened at noon, so be it. I changed my schedule accordingly. This really drove my ego mad! The internal chatter told me I was lazy and unproductive; I longed to go back to the 4 AM wake-up time. Predictability had set in, and the once uncomfortable had become comfortable.

One of the warrior's greatest strengths is his unpredictability and inaccessibility. This is directly due to the fact that, transcending the ego's desires, he refuses to allow himself to get locked into habitual patterns.

Remember that discipline always has been, and will continue to be, a key factor in the expansion of your consciousness and power. Do crazy things to break habitual routines–like taking ice-cold showers (this will really piss your ego off), eating when others are sleeping, and sleeping when others are awake. Move frequently, changing your environment and situation. Give away your favorite piece of clothing or furniture.

Remind yourself that you are committed to a life of power, not weakness.

For several years I have studied with a teacher in Peru. To study with him, I must hike and camp at 16,400 feet in the Andes Mountains for a period of up to two weeks. It doesn't matter how fit you are–it is hard to breathe at that altitude, particularly when you are used to life at sea level! But the path of power is a warrior's path... and it will never be crowded. Many times I must re-mind myself that I AM in charge, not my whiny, energy-vampire ego or my physical body, which wants to quit on the first day.

- Do you need a certain lifestyle, a level of comfort, predictability, or control for your happiness?

- How much energy do you expend daily on projecting and protecting your desired self-image?

- How much of your life is routine and lived in a rut?

As a spiritual energy field, all of these physical normalities are products of the weak and insecure ego being fully in charge.

Practice escalating your power by saying no to your insecure and needy ego. Operate from a higher awareness and connect with the one source that is your true identity.

Erase Your Personal History

PRINCIPLE TWO

ALL great traditions, including the Essenes, the Druids, the Brahmins, the Gnostics, indigenous shamans, Christian mystics, and a multitude of others, have had death rituals as a cornerstone to advancement. In the words of Jesus, "Except one be born anew, he cannot enter the kingdom of God" (JOHN 3:3). Contrary to popular dogma, this is not a ritual of confessing your sins and accepting someone outside yourself as your savior. You must be your own savior.

Remember, God is an energy field (Spirit), and so are you: "The kingdom of heaven (expansion) is within." So how is one truly enabled to tap into the spiritual power within their very being? Just like transcending the ego, dis-enabling your past is a powerful step.

Understand *you* don't have a past; your ego does. That past is nothing but a memory of your ego mind. I am not suggesting that things did not occur in your younger life; certainly, they did. However, occurrences are just that: occurrences. They have meaning only as you give them meaning; they exist only as you hold them in your memory right now. Hold them differently or release them altogether, and your life dramatically changes.

The world is full of those who want to blame their parents, society, upbringing, experiences and a myriad of other past issues for their present state of affairs. This is erroneous and illusionary, and the greatest thief of power in existence. While these issues may have an effect (as long as you buy into them), they will never control you.

Remember, the only meaning anything has in your life is the meaning you give it through your own judgment. Judgment and observation are two entirely different things. Judgment is imposing your thoughts about how things "should be" upon a neutral situation. Observation is just objective awareness of a neutral situation.

Many so-called bad situations in your past have brought you many wonderful strengths and experiences–I guarantee it–and on some level you already know this is true. The difference between a warrior and a wimp is that the warrior *observes* everything as an opportunity while the wimp *judges* everything as a blessing or a curse. Judgment is the ego in full swing.

Imagine yourself on the highway in a fast sports car... accelerate to about ninety miles per hour... now drive while looking in the rearview mirror, not through the windshield. A guaranteed disaster in the making, right? Yet how many people do you know who are driving into the future while focusing on the past?

In my early twenties, I had a buddy who owned a cigarette boat (one of those testosterone-filled, long, low, and ultra-fast speedboats). We would go out cruising the lake, looking as cool as possible and attempting to attract attention from the ladies.

As we screamed across the water with the nose of the boat in the air, I would often look behind as the powerful engines dug in and left a hefty wake. The first question I want you to consider is, "What is the wake?" Answer: It is nothing more than a trail left behind. Second question, "Can the wake ever drive the boat?" Obvious answer: no. Last question, "What drives the boat?" Most important answer: the energy of *the present* moment.

Is there a metaphor here? Yes, I think there is!

Your personal history is nothing more than the trail left behind. It has no inherent ability to drive your life any more than a wake can drive a boat. Notice I did not say that it *couldn't* drive your life, only that your personal history has no innate ability to define your destination.

Countless hours of therapy and large amounts of dollars could be saved if this truth of "wake" versus "present moment energy" were fully understood.

> **"No man, having put his hand to the plow, and looking back, is fit for the kingdom of God."**
> **–Luke 9:62**

If you *know* who you are, *really know*, you can erase your past in an instant. Change happens in an instant despite what most people think. Change often appears to be a long process, but everything preceding change is actually nothing but a ramp up to the instant of change. Isn't now a good time to stop being driven by your past?

Your past is ultimately illusion and exists only in your mind. However, since most people are not in full possession of this "knowing," I invest considerable time during my seminars assisting participants in releasing the energy drain of the past. Every moment you invest in looking back steals precious energy and vitality from your present.

In your journey of power, one of the most important activities in which you can be involved is the erasure of your past. The warrior who wields the greatest power is the one who has no personal history.

This is not really as bizarre as it may initially seem. Scientists now tell us that our *entire bodies* are replaced approximately every seven years. Every cell, bone, and organ is literally dying and re-birthing. With this knowledge you realize that the person you were seven years ago (or even fewer) no longer exists except in your mind.

Therefore, all the mistakes and experiences you had in your past in a very real sense *were not you*... unless you continue to be defined and attached to these dramas of mind!

Many people drain energy by focusing on the pain supposedly imposed by their past, just as many lose energy dreaming about the "good old days." Both viewpoints are equally limiting.

> **"They just sit around dreaming, talking about the old times, glory days."**
> **–Bruce Springsteen**

Just like letting go of the wake of pain, one of the most important decisions warriors make is to move on from environments and relationships they have outgrown. You must have the courage to move forward. Think of it as taking off an outfit that is worn out and no longer fits you. Be willing to let it go.

I have been something of a vagabond for much of my adult life. At one point, I moved five times in a three-year period. Although at first this may seem to be a superficial way to change, if practiced as a conscious discipline, it can prove powerful.

Let me go on record as saying I do not believe that moving to a new city will, in and of itself, change your life or save your relationships. I recall one distraught couple telling me they had decided to make a fresh start in a new city. I reminded them that although they might move to a new city, the two of them would still be there. This is a classic example of looking for answers in externals instead of through self-examination. Remember, the battle lies within.

In other words, moving does not in and of itself provide growth. For someone who has moved constantly to run away from problems, settling down in one place for a while would be a great way to shake up the ego.

As a warrior, with focused effort you can remold yourself and your identity in a move. At the same time, you can strategically and purposefully remove yourself from some habitual circles and environments. The key distinction is that *you* must become someone radically different.

For me, moving has been a ritual of letting go of the familiar, deciding how I am going to show up going forward, acknowledging who and what I am leaving behind, and taking my comfort-seeking ego off its pedestal.

Erasing your past is a commitment to condense your energy in the here and now. Power exists in the present moment–everything else exists only in your mind and is a drain of energy.

Let go of the idea that your parents, your school, your birth order, or any past experience make and/or define you. Let go of the energy vampires in your life–habits, environments, or relationships you have outgrown–and move on. Be willing to walk away from this limited living.

While there are many processes, rituals, and practices to erase your past (both modern and historical), ultimately your past is erased through sheer intent, commitment, and escalation of power.

According to Qabalah, the foundation of all western esoteric schools of thought, the sole reason you and I are here is to escalate our individual consciousness. This fact is completely aligned with all great spiritual, scientific, and evolutionary understandings.

The next great breakthrough for you in life is to re-member that you come from Spirit and are held in the Divine Mind as a perfect masterpiece. You did not conceive yourself: You have been perfectly conceived and are always held in the mind of the perfect Creative Source as a perfect being.

Everything has been chosen by and for you in this life journey for one purpose only–your growth and advancement. Frequently the most "difficult" life situations bring the greatest gifts.

When you experience this awakening, you will re-cognize (know again) the perfection of everything in this grand drama of your life, be thankful for it, pay homage to it, release it, and move on. Let the wake be the wake.

On a metaphysical and physical level, you will experience a tremendous surge of power and release. This is the true meaning of "being born anew."

Less Is More

PRINCIPLE THREE

THIS is a concept your ego will challenge, but the warrior realizes that power does not come from toys, trinkets, bobbles, and beads. In fact, the more things you have, the more your power is drained.

The paradox: Less is more, and more is less.

I am sure you have heard this in one way, shape, or form before, but do you really understand and live this paradox? The fact is that most people in Western society live life way beyond their financial means. Income falls severely short of outgo.

Every "thing" takes energy to maintain. The nicer the thing, typically the more attention and energy are necessary.

I remember my first egg-beater car in high school. I put very little energy into it beyond gas and oil. At one point I ran into a wall (that's a long story which we won't go into here) and crunched the fender. Instead of getting it fixed or letting my parents find out, I just rubbed thick mud on the dent and left it. Since I never washed the car, this plan worked beautifully–until it was eventually totaled. (Not even a field of mud could have saved it at that point!)

While there was energy expenditure on my first car, it was much minimized... but understand it was still there. Since I was no longer riding with my friends, I had to stop and buy gas, come up with the money to pay for the gas and oil, buy tires, park it somewhere, buy a key ring, remember where I placed my keys–the list goes on. Get the point? And the expenditure only escalates as the car gets nicer. It costs a fortune to run a Porsche–the car payments are just the beginning–not to mention the mental energies invested (finding a place to park where it won't get dinged, etc.).

You think it would be nice to have a certain home or nice car? Maybe. The payments are just the beginning of the endless expenditures and upkeep. And, ultimately, what will they give you? Will they bring joy, happiness, and power to you? Or will they become such energy expenditures that your possessions will eventually own you?

You actually own nothing, regardless of what society thinks. Every single thing you now possess will eventually belong to someone else. You are only a temporary custodian for as long as you are here in this form. Your home, even when paid for, will someday belong to someone else. Your car, your clothes, your jewelry–everything! Only that which is eternal has any true value. Keep that in mind when you begin to move into a potential energy deficit for that new trinket.

The warrior understands that energy is power and power is energy. You will never have full power if you are constantly leaking and expending your reserves. This is true mentally as well as physically.

The ego will never be satisfied, no matter what you have.

Get that dream car, house, toy, income, and be guaranteed that it will not be enough. Your small ego self will always want more. The more things you have, the more energy expenditures you have. As a result, the more you have to maintain, the more energy you have going out, and the more limited your reserves.

Furthermore, you cannot fully appreciate a myriad of things as much as you can appreciate one or two things. If you have one beautiful painting, you will definitely appreciate it more than if you have a whole house full of beautiful paintings. One or two nice things will feel more appreciated (and take less energy) than endless toys and trinkets. You have an absolute right to abundance, but you don't have a right to extravagance. There is a difference: Understand it and control it.

Do you control your needs or do your needs control you? Do you use your possessions or do they own and use you?

Make a commitment to a lifestyle greatly simplified.

As previously mentioned, I move my residence frequently, and for the last several years I have typically moved each year. While the move process is not always the most comfortable activity for my ego self, I enjoy the flexibility and non-attachment of letting material things go and exploring new places and environments. This pisses the ego off in the worst kind of way, due to the high value the ego places on comfort, control, and predictability. That's exactly what makes moving an action of power!

Another powerful practice encouraged by moving is cleaning out worthless accumulated junk in my closet and home. My recommendation is this: If you have not worn or used something for a year, get rid of it—even if it is brand new or was expensive! You are abundant, so there is no need to hold and hoard. Obviously the energy is gone from the object or you would be utilizing it on a regular basis. It is wasting space and stealing energy. Give these things to someone who will appreciate and utilize them.

And, by the way, don't do the petty garage sale thing. It doesn't matter if it is a couch or dinette or how much it cost you. Selling your old material goods is an activity of the small mind with a scarce and limited viewpoint. Give it away—*prove* to your small ego self that you are unlimited and abundant.

I am not suggesting you should not have or appreciate nice things—quite the contrary. I find it is much better to have a few really nice things that I appreciate rather than a whole house full of mediocre things that I don't. Less is more.

The difference between enjoyment and attachment is a vital understanding. Do you have something in your life right now that you absolutely believe you need? Something you are unwilling to let go of? If yes, then you are attached. Attachment (at any level) makes you weak. The warrior has the freedom to enjoy anything and everything, but if it goes, so be it–he is unfazed.

Make energy conservation and escalation your primary concern. The warrior stays lean and mean. In the words sung by Janis Joplin, "Freedom is just another word for nothing left to lose."

Become Self-Referring

B ECAUSE we live in a world focused on externals, we have developed into individuals who are object-identified. We have conditioned ourselves to think we are our things, jobs, titles, neighborhoods, salaries, relationships, reputation, and so on. Ask the question, "Who are you?" and ninety-nine times out of one hundred you will hear a definition centered on what a person *does* or what they *have*. If you are what you have, then when you have it no more you are no more. If you are what you do, then when you do it no more you are no more.

You are not what you do or have–you are more than that. You are not a mother or father–you *have* children. You are not an engineer, sales professional, accountant, lawyer, doctor–that is what you *do* for a living.

- Can you take a stand for what you believe in when everyone and everything else disagrees?

- How often do you act to make others happy or to be accepted?

- Do you attempt to "win people over?"

- Do you get upset when someone thinks poorly of you?

How you answer these questions determines if you are others-referred or self-referred, whether their opinions are more important to you than your own.

The path of power is one of understanding your own divinity and infinity. You can boldly state, "I am a child of the Creative Source on the journey of power." This does not mean that you make excuses for your shortcomings–far from it. It just means that when you are doing your best, you don't need anyone or anything to affirm you. You affirm yourself.

When I first began public speaking, I would give presentations and sometimes receive standing ovations. (By the way, I now understand that if you are getting standing ovations in your life, chances are great that you are not pushing people to think and grow. People usually applaud things with which they agree and are comfortable.)

Anyway, the entire audience may have loved me, but if one person approached and said something negative, it would ruin my high. Likewise, how many times have you purchased a gift for a friend or family member, invested a lot of energy, effort, and thought into it, and then they didn't like it? How did you feel? If you got your feelings hurt, it was because you became object-referred. You are not your Christmas gifts nor anything else that you obtain, possess, or do. You are so much more than that!

> Abraham Maslow stated that the highest level of self-actualization was "being beyond the good opinion of others."

Let go of the need to be externally accepted and supported. Let go of the need to be affirmed and made to feel important by toys and trinkets. Stand up–wake up–be a person of power! Step into your full power and re-member your divine and infinite identity.

Become Self-Reliant

C AN you sustain yourself without any support or assistance from others?

Can you thrive in an environment where no one will be with you, counsel you, or assist you?

The warrior walks the path of power. Consequently, he or she lives a life in which no one is indispensable. If you think this seems arrogant or cold, you are far from the truth. There is a major difference between "choosing" and "needing" something or someone. Let me give you a quick example.

Imagine that you have a daughter and you never teach her how to change a flat tire. Late one night she is out on the highway and the undesirable flat tire occurs. What now? She is totally at the mercy of whoever may or may not come along. Not a good place to be: She has no options and no choices. In other words, she is dependent.

Conversely, let's assume you teach her to change a flat and the same thing occurs. Now she has a choice. She may very well choose not to change the tire for fear of getting grease on her clothes, but she certainly can change the tire if no one else is available to do it for her. Now she is self-reliant.

There is a continuum from dependence to independence, followed by interdependence; each is a prerequisite of the next. In other words, you cannot be interdependent unless you are first independent. Dependence is a prison of one's own making, the realm of weakness and need. Independence is a level of self-reliance that knows you can drive your own bus, you are in charge of your own destiny, and you need no one and no thing to survive and thrive.

The highest level on the continuum is interdependence. This is a level of operation in which you understand that while you absolutely *can* make it alone, you choose to act and interact with others. You surround yourself with people who bring a wealth of experience, talents, and ideas into your life because your life is improved as a result.

Your first impression may be to think that you are currently operating at the highest levels but, please, do not fool yourself.

Honestly, what measure of aloneness can you sustain? Can you enjoy your personal relationships, yet be detached from neediness? *Can* you walk away if necessary?

The warrior can walk–any day, any time, any place.

The warrior is not attached or needy in any fashion. Do not make the mistake of thinking that this attitude is callous or unloving. Actually, the most loving and successful relationships on the planet, whether personal or business, are the result of two or more self-reliant, independent people coming together to form an unstoppable interdependence.

To become totally self-reliant truly takes experience–often the experience of ego discomfort and pain. In a very real sense, life is what happens to you when your ego is making other plans.

There have been countless times in my personal and business life in which my greatest challenge or most painful life-situation has catapulted me into a new realm. Remember that quantum leaps most often come after an ego death or a fall. I am sure in retrospect you also realize that some of your "most difficult times" have been some of your most amazing learning and growing experiences.

Power and self-reliance come from understanding this truth not in retrospect, but while under fire.

The great paradox is that while you are starring in your own story, you are also the extra in a grander production–maybe even acting a bit part in the divine play of life.

The insecure ego tends to attach to the familiar, convincing itself that it is needy and that it must predict and control. This place of weakness is a characteristic of the wet-paper-bag warrior versus the true warrior spirit.

You are infinite, and you don't need anyone or anything! Things may come and go, but you remain eternal. True power is a degree of self-reliance that *knows* "no matter what comes or goes, I will prevail."

This self-reliance has nothing to do with being cocky or making a loud-mouthed declaration. If you have to talk about it, you probably aren't self-reliant. Take notice of those who are always talking a big game: Without fail, you will find that they are attempting to convince you and themselves of something that is not there. When you have the power, there is nothing more to say.

Warriors with power have a quiet self-reliance that respects and loves others. They choose to interact with other powerful beings to bring diversity and wealth to the life journey–silently *knowing* that they never need.

Stand tall, warrior... step into your full power!

Realize Your Spiritual Identity

PRINCIPLE SIX

BEFORE we dive into this powerful principle, please do not confuse spirituality with religion. Spirituality is your one-on-one internal relationship with your Creative Source. Religion, on the other hand, is a collection of ideas, rules, and principles as to how to live a good life and obtain this individual relationship.

In the East, they tend to study the forest... in the West, we tend to count the trees. Don't miss the forest for the trees, my warrior friend.

Traditional religion often follows a business model (with a few exceptions) that is extremely outdated and centered on control. As religion became a corporate entity, dogma and compliance took precedence over the individual heroic quest. Multitudes have been conditioned into meaningless rituals (by those often utilizing fear as their prime motivating factor), all in the name of God.

Think about this: The primary objective for both Jesus and Buddha was not to enforce dogma and rules, but instead to assist you in remembering the divinity of man.

I am in no way advocating the eradication of churches or religion, but to add value in a modern world, they must radically update and change. The church of the future will be a laboratory of consciousness, housing a tribe of individuals committed to tracking power. These individuals will not study stories about sages of days gone by, but will have as their primary objective the pursuit of *becoming* the sage.

It's often been said, "You are not a human being having a spiritual experience; you are a spiritual being having a human experience." You are a spiritual being, an individual manifestation of the One Creative Source and Power, and this is your sole identity. The Essene tradition (to which Jesus was at minimum exposed) states, "The greatest sin is to question your divinity."

Spirit is always for fuller expression and expansion, and as a spiritual being you are here to expand and grow, period!

One of the challenges faced by average individuals is recognizing that they currently operate from an incorrect focus and definition of who they are and what the world is. There are three points of focus from which you have the ability to operate. My teacher, as well as many ancient traditions, calls these the "rings of power."

The first ring of power is the consensual world and all of its tangible entities. While operating in this world may seem natural and normal, it actually takes a tremendous amount of power (energy) just to hold together. The reason it appears to be simple is that you were conditioned to observe this world from the time of your birth, so it *seems* natural. You hold your world together with your attention—if you shift your attention, the world you know ceases to exist.

The second ring of power is the intangible world of Spirit. The warrior learns to step into this world of non-ordinary consciousness through the escalation of energy. There are several practices to assist you in exploring the realms of the second ring, but to do this takes a tremendous amount of focus and discipline.

The third and final ring of power is the ability to merge the two worlds. Once you are initiated into this third stage, you have the ability to operate from either or both by choice and at will.

Modern science is now confirming what mystics have known since time immemorial.

The greatest mistake is the belief that you are a solid physical entity. Physicists corroborate that what appears to be solid is actually 99.99999 percent space–or what the initiate knows as Spirit. For example, we once thought the atom to be solid. Now we know that if an atom were enlarged to the size of a football field, the nucleus of that atom would be a grain of rice on the fifty-yard line, with all electrons being additional grains of rice flying around the stadium. Obviously, you have a lot of space left over!

Initiates view themselves as fields of energy operating within a much larger field of energy. Power is determined by the amount of energy you are able to collect, condense, and escalate (CCE for short). The degree and level at which you can CCE directly determines your personal power.

To accelerate your energy to higher frequency and velocity, you must experience higher and higher levels of consciousness. This is not a situation where you can sit, listen, and learn. You may intellectually tell me, "Man, I am infinite," and you might truly believe this. You could listen to me tell you of your infinity as long as the day lasts, and once again believe it. But you will never *know* you are infinite until you have a direct personal experience of your higher infinite self. A major contributor to spiritual growth is the ability to traverse non-ordinary states of consciousness. Only in this way do you begin to dis-identify with your finite, physical self. You must step boldly into the second ring of power! Any spiritual institution that has hopes of thriving as the collective consciousness advances must facilitate the advance into the second ring.

Spiritual institutions must build their identity not as the end-all and be-all of truth, but begin to see themselves as centers of research; as a collective lab focused on the personal pursuit and experience of higher consciousness. Like any great institute of learning, spiritual research centers must seek to make themselves unnecessary. Any institution that does not propagate freedom and self-reliance is in error.

The book of John quotes Jesus as saying, "God is Spirit, and those who worship him must worship in Spirit."

Notice he never said that God is some great white man on a throne in the sky who will grant your wishes if you are a good boy or girl. Nor did he ever say that if you live your life extremely well, obeying all the rules, you will earn a condo on a cloud.

All of these childish thoughts come from the finite mind of man attempting to explain (and therefore humanize) infinite spiritual concepts. The second ring of power is a leap into the world of Spirit. This leap is the higher state of which all teachers and traditions have spoken.

The word "heaven" comes from the original Greek word *ouranos*, meaning "expansion" or "to expand." Therefore, the "heaven" that the mind of man has turned into a palace on a cloud (with golden streets, and every citizen issued white robes and wings) is actually the kingdom of expansion: In other words, the evolution and expansion of your own personal consciousness and power.

What Jesus did say is, "The kingdom of heaven is within," and "The kingdom of heaven is at hand." Both of these statements clearly communicate that you must go inside to access your expansive power–and the time to harness it is now.

Remember, God is Spirit, and this Spirit is within. Your very identity is Spirit; you can't be anything other than that from whence you came. The beginning of all that exists is Spirit, and consequently, you are one with all persons and things. Do you choose to have more in your life? Do you desire more power? If you do, the source lies within, and to access it you must first recognize your identity. You are a spiritual energy field on a mission of expansion. Realize your spiritual identity and step into the second ring of power!

Seek first the kingdom of expansion, and all things will be given to you.

Become a Serious Student

You have a whole host of beliefs that were handed to you at a very early age: beliefs about the Creative Source, the world, right and wrong, good and bad, yourself. Beliefs drive your behavior in every moment of every day, yet most of your beliefs are not backed up by experiences or personal references. In other words, they are most often unsolicited gifts from people in your life and environment.

We are all born seekers, but very few of us become students. As a person of power, you are a student of the grandest magnitude: Never taking anything at face value, you pursue your own truth and your own personal experience.

The warrior questions *everything*! For years, I have had a question mark made out of crystal sitting on a carved stone stand upon my desk to constantly remind me of this practice.

Traditional religion, school systems, and the government have conditioned you to the contrary. Consider the individual who is rewarded most highly in our school system. The teacher's pet is never the creative thinker, rather the person who complies most fully with all the rules.

We are taught to "have faith" and to "believe" by those people in positions of power (often granted by some document, degree, or committee), who frequently have very little of their own personal experience of the Creative Source, yet to question their authority has historically been damnable.

One of the most attractive features I have experienced in shamanic traditions is that the shaman is a tracker of power (a serious student). His insights are derived from a direct revelation/personal experience of the transcendent source. Understand that the term *shaman*, like Christ or Buddha, is a title indicating an enlightened state of consciousness. The shaman of any tradition explores and communes frequently in altered reality and higher consciousness, and is never appointed, awarded, or elected.

Beliefs are of the intellect and, while they have their place in the evolutionary ladder, they are glowsticks for children when compared to personally tapping into high voltage. All great initiates have been serious students at one point in their journeys, but once the foundation is laid, there is always a shift and enlightenment is received through self-revelation. The ultimate teacher is higher consciousness itself.

At some point in your journey, you must become your own teacher. To do this, you must first and foremost become a serious student and dedicate your life to the path of power. Few are willing to do what it takes to pursue this path, and there is a major difference between being "interested" and being "committed." Many have the *interest* to explore and dabble, but few have the *commitment* necessary to follow through. As stated earlier, to get on the path is commendable–to stay on the path is unique indeed.

> **No college degree or intellectual exercise can substitute for personally plugging into the second ring of transcendent power.**

The Buddha used to tell his new students of a widowed father with one son. While away on a business trip, thieves entered and burned his home, kidnapping his son. The father returned to find his house burned to the ground and what appeared to be the charred remains of his only son. Heartbroken, he gathered the ashes and placed them in a beautiful urn that never left his side.

After some time passed, the son escaped from the kidnappers and returned home to his father. Approaching his father's house late in the evening, he knocked on the door. The father, awakening from a deep sleep, called out, "Who is it?" His son replied, "It is me, father, your son." The grief-stricken father shouted in anger for him to go away, thinking that a cruel child was playing a prank. After much effort, but to no avail, the son left, never to return again.

After this story, the Buddha would tell his new students, "Sometimes you buy into something so strongly as truth that when truth comes to you in person and knocks on your door, you will not let it in."

- How many of your beliefs are your own?

- How many of them qualify as "knowing" from a direct personal experience?

- How open are you to questioning everything you believe to be true?

The serious student is open and flexible, realizing that rigidity can allow higher truth to knock at your door, yet be denied.

The tracker of power must learn to question everything–to let go of the childish. Where did this idea, habit, belief come from? Do I have direct personal experience of this, or was it handed to me as a gift from my mommy or daddy? Does the person I am listening to exhibit true power–can I see powerful results in this person's life? Do I aspire to create the same results? Does this belief serve me, or has it worn out its welcome?

"Judge not that you be not judged." You have most likely been *conditioned to believe* that this is speaking of some great "judgment day" at the end of the world. However, understand that judgment is nothing more than placing your own opinions onto someone or something. You can only and always project outside of yourself what is *inside* yourself–you cannot give what you don't have. Since we are all one, any judgment you give to situations or others is the judgment that resides in you, and you bestow that same gift upon yourself.

One practice of the serious student is what I will call the "movie mindset." Most people watching a movie willingly suspend their disbelief of what is transpiring for the two-hour period. For instance, you will never enjoy a James Bond movie if you are constantly saying or thinking, "There is no way that could really happen." If you want to get your money's worth of entertainment, you suspend what you know for the duration of the film, and just take it in, experience it, and go with the flow. After the conclusion, if you choose to analyze the movie you can, but in the meantime you enjoyed the experience. This is the movie mindset and a great way to live and experience the adventure of life.

The serious student has a child-like openness and willingness to learn: a curious movie mindset focused on complete enjoyment. The know-it-alls of the world, those individuals who are too rigid and unwilling to question anything, are caught in the throes of the insecure and fearful ego and will never step into their full power.

Einstein said, "When you appoint yourself as judge and jury of truth and righteousness, you are shipwrecked by the laughter of the gods." One of the most powerful tools in my own life experience has been my willingness to be tutored. I am able to be open and to subjugate myself to a teacher or mentor, not in worship, but in appreciation of the principle and power that the teacher represents.

Are you willing to question that which you think is true? Are you willing to suspend your disbelief and be open to the truth that may be knocking on your door? Or will you send it away, prove yourself right, and remain where you currently reside for the rest of your life?

I challenge you to become a serious student and live a life of power–you will be glad you did.

Become a Metaphysician
Principle Eight

THIS principle warrants some explanation. If the word *metaphysical* concerns or threatens you, it is probably due to an incorrect definition. The prefix *meta-* means to rise above or go beyond. Therefore, anything metaphysical is above and beyond the physical plane of existence.

To become a metaphysician is to become a student of cause and effect. There is a metaphysical reason for *every* physical result. As you step into your spiritual identity and become a serious student of the second ring of power, this axiom of cosmic principle becomes self-evident. Understanding this axiom and living it are two different matters. Living by non-physical principles takes great amounts of commitment, discipline, and personal power.

The first step in metaphysics is to turn away from the appearances produced by sensory data. While this is difficult, you already practice this—and you have for some time. If you lived entirely by your sensory data, you would believe that the earth was flat and standing still. Yet at this point in history, you are informed enough to know that the earth is round and hurtling through space.

Your senses tell you that there is water on the highway ahead of you as you drive across the desert... but you know better. Your senses tell you that the sun takes a bath in the ocean at night and burrows through the earth to break through the next morning.

Your senses tell you that railroad tracks meet in the distance, that dog whistles make no sound, that music you hear on the radio is produced by the box, and the list goes on.

Your senses also inform you that the actions you do or do not take in your daily life are the cause of all that you produce or lack: physical reasons for physical results. I submit that, just as with all the examples before, when it comes to observing *cause* and how results are produced, your senses are a poor gauge of reality.

While you may have the ability to understand some of these examples of visual and auditory illusion, it is much more difficult to know that in reality you are the creator of everything that manifests in your life. Yes, everything! And this creative power is beyond any physical activity.

It was Socrates who stated, "The unexamined life is not worth living," and as a serious student your primary studies must concentrate on your own inner world. As a metaphysician you must become an explorer of inner space. The more deeply you dive into realms only explored by champions, the more you will understand true cause in all of its grandeur.

> **Your outer world and all of its manifestations
> are nothing more than a reflection of your
> inner world—as within, so without.**

One of the most profound passages in the Bible relating to metaphysics is in the book of Proverbs. It states, "As you think so shall you be." Notice it does not state, "As you be so shall you think," yet many live their lives as "be-then-think" people, allowing their thoughts to be totally defined and driven by external sensory data. An animal can do that!

Animals by and large live their lives completely by sensory data. However, you know someone in your life right now (did you catch yourself falling into the trap?) living with no more power than an animal. Those who buy into this animalistic mindset are complete wet-paper-baggers, living as victims of their own making when they could be victors. Do not allow externals to write your life story.

There are two levels to any game you play: the external and the internal. In the game of tennis, for example, there is the external game consisting of the forehand, backhand, and serve. There is also an internal game consisting of the vision, self-belief, self-identity, determination, commitment, and follow-through. Now consider which one drives results more fully–the inner game or the outer game? The answer is the inner game, the primary determiner of all our outer actions and results.

As a metaphysician, your first expedition must be in the field of thought. (Eventually you will move beyond the level of thought as well, but let's take one step at a time.) To change performance in any area, you must first change your own thinking.

In the beginning phases of your journey of power, it will be vitally important that you:

· Become a voracious reader.

· Find a mentor, coach, or teacher.

People, Us Weekly, Reader's Digest, and fictional novels do not qualify as material for voracious reading. All leaders are great readers. Find a person of power (they will be easy to spot in this world of mass mentality) who can point you in the right direction when it comes to what to read. Commit to reading a minimum of one good book a month. This practice alone will transform your thinking and, therefore, your world. Be transformed by the renewal of your mind.

I personally had read hundreds of books in a variety of fields–all great religions, philosophy, psychology, personal development, and quantum physics–prior to ever attracting my most profound teachers. The adage, "When the student is ready the teacher will appear" has proven to be absolutely true for me.

I was recently conducting my Quantum Leap seminar in which I mentioned one of my teachers. A young enthusiast rushed up to me during the break and asked, "How did you find your teacher? I need to find someone just like that!" I immediately answered, "I attracted him into my life," then asked, "How many books have you read? How long have you studied? How many years have you invested? How many seminars have you attended? Most important, what have you put into practice that you have learned?"

When you are able to answer those questions powerfully, then you will find the right teacher "magically" appearing in your life.

Be humble and open.

Let me coach you that when you find your teacher, be willing to do whatever necessary to learn from him or her. I have flown across the North American continent on many occasions to spend a few hours with one of my teachers. As stated before, I have even traveled out of the country, incurring great financial expense and physical hardship when necessary. Be willing.

Second, never attempt to impress your teacher with all that you know. This is a behavior of the ego looking to get stroked, admired, or accepted. I know many "could be" powerhouses who cannot put their ego aside long enough to allow themselves to be taught.

I recommend you plan on taking a spiritual (metaphysical) journey at least once per year. Either go alone, with a small group of like-minded students, or with a teacher who is truly conscious and dialed in. We all need support and assistance to pull ourselves from the quagmire of the collective vibration. We need to be reminded at regular intervals. To be a person of power, you absolutely must invest the time to step out of the mundane and experience a higher energy state. While books and learning systems are wonderful, they will never replace the impact of the face-to-face experience. Accomplish this experience by visiting a sacred site of power or by studying with a teacher of higher consciousness. Both sacred sites and true teachers are incredible energy vortices, and merely being exposed to these higher vibrations can change you profoundly.

You must have an immersion learning experience at a minimum of once per year.

After approximately twenty years of reading, traveling, and being coached, I realized that my greatest learning came from tapping directly into the Creative Source from which we all originate. The daily conditioning is what separates the dreamer from the achiever. While I am still excited to read, study and attend events designed for learning (and still do), my greatest return comes from my times of quiet and solitude.

It stands to reason that to become a metaphysician you must at some point have an experience of something other than the physical. Many of my teachers have helped me in this realm, but I know that their assistance would not have had nearly the same effect if I was not committed to my own daily practice.

You have a metaphysical energy or astral body that is a double of your physical body. Depending on the degree of power you do or do not possess, you can traverse between the two. Furthermore, the more time invested in the realms of higher consciousness, the more powerful your astral body becomes. Many displays of "miracles" have been the result of the great sages operating in the astral/etheric state–residing beyond the physical realm. The creative energy substance, the primeval source from which every form manifests, is not physical.

All great traditions have had their rituals, rites of passage, and altered states of consciousness. It is not the purpose of this writing to instruct you in ways to access these higher realms. Many of my live events and learning systems are designed to assist with experiencing these kingdoms of power. However, it is important to know that if you long to soar beyond the mundane, you must do so in the inner sanctuary of the most high. In other words, you must go into the inner space and shut the door behind you. While I (and others) may assist you in getting there, you ultimately must go alone. Your ego will fight you all the way, so be prepared. The birth of a new level of consciousness will necessitate an ego transcendence, and we have previously discussed the difficulties this presents.

There in the depths of your own consciousness, you will find your most dangerous enemy–and only there will you learn to master it. Please understand that if you can't dance with your own demons, you will never walk in the light.

> **When the dance is done, you will find your true spiritual self, your wisest teacher and best adviser.**

There in the power of silence, you will find God Spirit in the deepest part of your being. Only then will you know the unity of God Spirit and man. You will finally understand and *know* in what image you are created–not because you read it in some document, but because you *experienced* it! Only then will you realize that in lack of consciousness alone has there been a separation between Creator and creation. Only in appearances has there been duality–just as our spirit, mind, and physical bodies have appeared to be separate.

Only then will you not judge by appearances. Then you will experience and *know* that in reality you and the creative power are one. You will realize that the gateway to heaven (expansion) is through your own consciousness. This is the vision of the ladder revealed to Jacob in the Old Testament, which the initiate must ascend before entering into that silent palace of power. The gates are open and waiting; you must take the first step!

Be Committed and Willing

PRINCIPLE NINE

THIS is what separates the champion from the masses. As we discussed earlier, we are all born seekers–but very few of us become students.

Siddhartha Gautama exited his palace walls, left his wife and children, and committed himself to finding the solution to end all suffering. He invested the next twenty-one years of his life traveling far and wide, studying with many masters and teachers, practicing a multitude of difficult processes and rites of passage. He fasted until he could literally count the vertebrae in his spine from the front side of his body. Finally he arrived at the foot of a Bodhi tree and vowed not to leave until the answer was revealed. It was here that his breakthrough of consciousness was achieved and he became the Buddha.

You may be aware that the Bible is missing thirty full years of the life of Jesus. What do you think he was doing during that time, fishing? Hardly. He was becoming the Christ.

With the discovery of the Dead Sea Scrolls, it has been surmised that Jesus most likely studied with the Essenes, a secret brotherhood well-known for rigorous physical, mental, and spiritual rites of passage. Jesus was advancing his consciousness and preparing for thirty years prior to his three-year mission that would impact the world for eternity.

When the modern guru Bubba Free John first approached his teacher, he was overweight and out of work. He asked, "Can you teach me the secrets of enlightenment?" to which his teacher replied, "Go lose twenty pounds and get a job." Bubba Free John went and did as asked: He was willing. Upon his triumphant return, he asked his teacher the same question and received the response, "Pick up that broom and sweep the floor." This is where it all began for one of today's most revered teachers, someone whom theology expert Alan Watts has called an avatar, the real thing.

One of my teachers is a Qu'ero Indian. The Qu'ero populate the high country of the great Andes Mountains and are the last direct descendents of the Inca. There are only approximately four hundred of the Qu'ero left alive. His apprentices have studied with him for eighteen years and are still not full-fledged initiates into his order.

I was first attracted to my studies of ancient traditions after reading many of the great works of Carlos Castaneda and his teacher, don Juan. Castaneda tells how after studying with don Juan for several years, his teacher decided it was time to test his true commitment.

Don Juan told Carlos that he must give away everything he owned, leave all of his friends, and check into a seedy hotel. He must stay there until he no longer cared if anyone came to visit him nor if he lived or died. The requirement was to stay as long as necessary, but it must be for a minimum of three months. This was the only way to prove that he was able to transcend his ego and move to the next level of power.

Castaneda told him he that he could not do this, to which don Juan replied, "That's fine. It has been nice knowing you, and I wish you well," and he left. Castaneda was interested, but not committed.

After some months without his teacher, he realized what he had lost, reconsidered, and followed through.

I recall some years ago there was a supposed avatar from the East conducting a weekend retreat in San Francisco. An avatar is an individual who fully embodies the divine, and some say avatars are born fully enlightened. (I now realize there is no such thing... *everyone* has to do the work.)

I was not certain that this person would be who the claims stated he was, but I went as a serious student with an open mind.

When I first arrived, I was directed to a barracks-type room with a lot of other people and assigned to the kitchen for dish detail throughout the entire weekend. In the Eastern tradition this was to be my gift to the teacher.

At the time I was living in the lap of luxury in La Jolla, California, thinking myself quite successful and consciously advanced. You might imagine the internal dialogue my ego was having as I received this less-than-auspicious welcome. My small self did not want to sleep in a dorm and certainly didn't want to wash dishes–I wanted the Ritz Carlton! But I decided to stick it out.

When the meeting began, we were gathered in a large room with no chairs and were directed to sit on the concrete floor with hundreds of others to wait for the great teacher. Not knowing the drill, I was unprepared and didn't have my own pad and floor-sitting paraphernalia like those in-the-know had brought–major bummer. Three hours passed and no teacher arrived. My legs and back were screaming with discomfort, and I was questioning my own sanity. I also was beginning to question the others in attendance–"If they are so damn spiritual why aren't they sharing their pillows and pads with me?!"

My funk was on a roll and gaining momentum.

When the teacher arrived, everyone got on their knees and bowed their foreheads to the floor–this sucked! And it was almost the last straw for my whiny ego-self. I was just about to exit stage left when something from my higher nature said, "What if...? Just what if this person is who they claim? Would it be worth the price of the physical pain and discomfort? Would it be worth swallowing my pride?"

I spent the next two hours crawling on my knees, edging forward in single file, one inch at a time, to get to the feet of the teacher. Avatar or not, there was a tremendously powerful loving energy emanating from this being that I remember clearly to this day. It definitely affected me. But just as important (if not more so) was the impact of the humbling of self and my willingness to pay the price even when my ego screamed. I am glad I did.

> **There is always a price for the prize, and you are either willing to pay it or you are not. Most people are not.**

Once again, the path of power is a warrior's path, and it will *never* be crowded. What are you willing to invest for the unimaginable return? Are you willing to do whatever it takes? Are you willing to forsake all for the chance of a lifetime?

Please don't fool yourself into thinking the warrior's path is easy. It is not–nor is it supposed to be. If it were easy, then everyone would be an initiate of the highest order. All are called, but few hear the call; even fewer complete the journey. Are you interested or committed? Think clearly, my friend, because I assure you that your commitment will be tested.

The incredible advancement of every great sage, teacher, and saint since time immemorial resulted from their commitment and willingness to do whatever necessary to achieve the highest stages of consciousness.

Likewise, every one of them has told us they are not an isolated case but rather an example of perfected man. Jesus said, "Even the least among you can do all that I have done... and even greater things."

My friends often ask, "What the heck are you doing trekking around the Andes? Flying off to far-away places and investing so much time and money? Don't you have a business to run?" They obviously just don't get it.

I understand, though: Many times in the throes of exhaustion or frustration I have asked myself the same questions. (This most frequently occurs when I am asked to do something my wimpy ego doesn't like.) But I continue on, and so must you.

Count the costs before beginning the journey, my interested friend; you will be tested. Are you truly committed? Are you willing to pay the price for the prize beyond measure? If truly committed, you will find that the horizons, the experiences, and the power are ineffable. Hang on and fasten your seat belt–you are in for an amazing ride!

Find Comfort in Discomfort

EVERYTHING in our world, from plants to people, is in a state of transition. There is no standing still: You are either growing or dying. A plant is either blossoming, blooming, unfolding–or it is fading, withering, dying away. Nothing remains the same–and what is true of nature is true of you.

When people say to me, "I wish things would be the way they used to be" or "I wish this change would hurry up and get over with so that things get back to normal," they are revealing their ignorance of a fundamental truth.

You are a spiritual being, and spirit has only one objective: fuller expression and expansion. Spirit is never for stagnation or contraction. As a result, you must realize that the *only* time you are comfortable is when you are doing something you have already done. You are comfortable only with repeats–not with record-breaking. Repeats are indicators of death–your higher self wants you to grow!

We already have discussed the great traditions' recognition that advances in consciousness almost always follow a "fall" or an ego death/transcendence. You can take personal inventory of your growth in direct proportion to your "falls."

Ego falls and transcendent possibilities come in all shapes and sizes. Almost without exception, situations like divorce, death of a loved one, illness, losing a job, bankruptcy, or business crises all make you a kinder, humbler, more loving person. I am sure you agree that some of your greatest life gifts and learning came disguised as catastrophes.

I wrote an article some time ago entitled, "Relationships are the Zen of the Western World." Relationships have an uncanny ability to show you to yourself. It is really easy to be the Buddha when you are sitting alone in your living room, but put yourself in a laboratory with a kitchen and den (also known as a home) with another research subject (also known as your mate), and things begin happening that test how enlightened you really are.

Spiritual teacher Ram Dass aptly stated, "If you think you are really enlightened, go spend a week with your parents." While relationships are not the only cause of discomfort, they provide a tremendous opportunity for you to push the envelope. Relationships of all shapes and sizes create a friction, a discomfort that allows you the opportunity to see yourself in all your glory (or lack thereof), if you are open and willing.

Coming from a staunch traditional Christian background, I began studying Buddhism and practicing meditation in my early twenties after "the woman of my dreams" dropped me like a hot rock. My life was "over," and I needed to find solace. What I found was a study and practice that has served me every day since that so-called fall.

The spiritual student views life from a higher perspective, thereby developing the powerful skill of seeing every situation and circumstance as a gift, even if disguised. Every difficulty creates an opportunity to grow and expand, even if you must do so with the ego kicking and screaming.

A totally predictable, controlled, and comfortable life would bore you out of your mind.

Learn to value excitement and adventure. Predictability is the food of wimps, not warriors. Predictability is death, and the life of power has no stomach for it. I recommend that you suck it up and go passionately in pursuit of your own discomfort. The only way to live is to grow—you can't fight change, so you might as well embrace it and charge forward.

Be Unique
PRINCIPLE ELEVEN

THE battle to be unique is the most difficult battle you will ever fight. The world around you will marshal every force at its command to keep you the same–also known as stuck. This is a battle that never ends.

In the movie *Autumn in New York*, starring Richard Gere and Winona Ryder, Ryder plays an unusual young woman who falls in love with an older man (played by Gere). In one scene, Ryder's character states to Gere's, "My mother always told me that I was 'a unique.' You, on the other hand, would be 'a normal.' " And this was obviously not meant to be a compliment.

Few individuals could realistically be considered "a unique" in the world–nor are they encouraged to be. Since the time you were small, you were not taught to be creative; you were taught to comply. Most probably, you have cultivated a need to "fit in," to be "a normal."

To live a life of impact, you must be willing to be unique in comparison to the collective consciousness. I am constantly looking for the misfits, mavericks, and outsiders of the world, whom I lovingly call the "MMOS." These people are not radicals proposing anarchy, but a group of individuals who think and operate from a higher order and state of consciousness.

MMOS pay their taxes, hold regular jobs, go to work each day: Judging by appearances, they seem to be just like the rest of society. But underlying it all there is a fundamental internal difference. These brave warriors are fully engaged yet detached. My teacher once told me, "James, you can play the game, but don't ever buy in."

The MMOs of the world are playing full-on but not buying in. What about you?

· Do you believe in traditional institutions, goals, and values, or do you see them for what they truly are?

· Does your philosophy of life belong to you, or is it borrowed and conditioned from the lowlands of the collective?

Little by little, day by day, person by person, these unique MMOs are gathering in momentum and numbers. The Buddha said, "Enlightenment is nothing more than progressive disillusion." The warrior MMOs are disillusioned with the current system, and they refuse to buy in.

Most often, the ranks of the MMOs are growing with the presence of those who are becoming fed up with "the system" and disenchanted with the values it propagates. I am not by any means advocating that you renounce or become a recluse–quite the contrary.

Always remember that while your identity is spiritual, your current membership is physical. That means you must play full-on in whatever profession or endeavor you choose. No one lives a life of power at half throttle.

Someone once asked me during a conference call, "James, if the Dalai Lama were running a race, do you think he would run to win?" I haven't got a clue what the big DL would do, but I know that from a warrior's standpoint, anything worth doing is worth doing one hundred percent, full-on. Yes, run to win... but don't base your identity or happiness upon the outcome.

The secret of power lies in running the race because *you choose* to run the race. Running the race because "everybody" is running, or because someone else wants you to run the race, or because "you should" run the race are not reasons from power, but reasons from weakness. Running for the acknowledgment or the prize is the ego domain of the collective. Run for the joy of running. If you win the trinket, that's nice. If you don't win the trinket, you still win. Have the courage to be unique: If the world thinks you a misfit, maverick, or outsider–so be it! The path of power will never be crowded!

Choose your own unique path and go for it.

"Should do's" are what other people desire you to do–bowing to them means you're not living from self-referral. How many people do you know who are always saying, "I should do this... I should do that"? Notice that any time you are stating a "should," you are not stating something that you are really passionate and excited about.

Many full-grown adults are still attempting to please their parents, even when their parents are dead. Your parents did the best they could with what they had available to them, but they have their life and you have yours.

Also, don't worry about what the neighbors think–in most cases they don't think at all! They are operating out of the collective conditioning that has been handed down generation after generation. Always remember, it is nobler to pursue your own passion imperfectly than to perfectly pursue someone else's.

Live your own life, and live it in your own way. Be unique!

Hold Yourself to a Higher Standard

PRINCIPLE TWELVE

PEOPLE of true impact always *give more* and *do more* than expected. The wet-paper-baggers always attempt to cut corners or, at best, do just enough to get by. There is *no way* to get ahead in life or live a life of power if you cut corners or do just enough.

If anything is worth doing, it is worth doing one hundred percent, giving your entire mind, body, and spirit to the effort. Anything worth doing is worth doing *big*. The more you give, the more you will receive.

How many times have you observed individuals putting out a little and expecting to get a lot in return? You know it doesn't work that way–don't fall into this lazy and weak ego trap.

All great initiates have told you to hold yourself to a higher standard in one way or another. One great teacher stated, "When someone asks for your shirt, give him your coat as well. When asked to carry something for a mile, carry it for two." What do you think was really being said? Is it only to be taken literally? I don't think so! This is a metaphor for the life of power, and for a characteristic of greatness. This is a message to give more than expected.

Greatness comes early and stays late: When others have decided that enough has been done, the warrior spirit is just getting started. This is true in work as well as in all other areas in the life of power.

To live a life of power, you must hold yourself to a standard higher than *anyone* else expects of you. Other people's standards will give you other people's results. Your standards, on the other hand, will create your destiny.

We have discussed the price that must be paid for any prize. I challenge anyone to find a person of power, in any area, who has not made great sacrifices and has not committed to tremendous discipline. If you ever hope to reach your full greatness, you must be committed. Count the costs before you begin the journey.

Holding yourself to higher standards is about taking full responsibility for everything in your life–yes, everything.

The power to create resides on the "at cause"–not the "at effect"–side of the equation.

- Do you take full responsibility for everything in your life? Good as well as not so good?

- Are you a passenger in life, or are you belted into the passenger seat?

- Do you step up and claim your own results... or do you often tell excuses and stories?

Warriors never explain or complain. They hold themselves much too high for that. When something goes less than stellar, warriors say, "Yes, I created that." They learn and go on.

When warriors are criticized, they remain silent. Remember what Eleanor Roosevelt said: "No one can make you feel inferior without your consent."

If the results you create are powerful, they speak for themselves. If warriors are applauded, they acknowledge it and realize that applause, too, shall pass. Playing the game but not buying in, they are never swayed.

If the result is less than desirable, you must claim it, learn from it, apply the learning, and move on. Period. Beating yourself up, feeling guilty or regretful about something that occurred, is wasted energy. The past is in concrete–never waste your time trying to chip away at it. Let the dead of spirit play with the dead.

The wet-paper-baggers are toxic complainers. Stay away from them–they are energy vampires and will suck the life right out of you. No one wants to be around them and, until a radical change takes place, they will never possess any real power. Nothing is ever right; nothing is ever good enough; nothing is ever complete; nothing is ever perfect.

The person on the path recognizes everything as perfect: All is possibility and challenge, an opportunity to learn, expand, and grow. Perfection is a state of mind–hold to a higher standard.

If you are constantly holding perfection as a set of rules, regulations, situations, and outcomes external to you, you will look in the mirror in the morning and the energy vampire in your life will be looking back. Go ahead, brush those fangs! If you are *really* in vampire mode, others will see this about you, but you will not. (Vampires have no reflection in a mirror, remember?) If people in your life start showing up with garlic, it might be time to check yourself out.

Okay, so you can step up to accountability for all your results. Now it's time to take higher standards to the next level. Years ago, when beginning my study of the tradition of Huna (the ancient Hawaiian spiritual teachings), I was encouraged by my teacher to step fully into the cause side of the equation. I had gotten somewhat comfortable with being at cause for all my results, so it was time for the next challenge. The ancient traditions teach that everything appearing in your world is of your own creation. This means that if a catastrophic weather event occurs in your world, you must ask yourself, "What did I do to create this?" or "Why did I attract this into my world model? What is it here to show and/or teach me?"

Now, whether you can intellectually get your mind around this concept or not is irrelevant. But if you can act as if you do, you will receive tremendous insights and power.

While this is often uncomfortable to the whiny ego, it has proven powerful beyond measure. I still ask myself the questions my teacher taught me: What in my life benefits from this event? When an earthquake occurs in California, you must ask, "How did I create this? What in my life needs shaking up? What is this telling me? What is the omen here?"

For instance, in one year of my life, three people in my circle of family and friends died or were diagnosed with a serious illness. By my training, I was called to ask myself, "What in me needs to die? What in me is unhealthy?"

Whether you believe you are actually the cause of all that happens around you or not doesn't really matter; the power is in getting the learning out of every event. See meaning and messages in everything that happens.

Any time you think the problem in your life is "out there," *that very thought* is a problem. You are giving your power away.

If your problem is the result of other people, the economy, situations, your workload, or anything outside of yourself, you are totally powerless. So if you think someone else is the problem in your life, should you send *them* through my JOURNEY OF POWER curriculum? Do you think *you* will get better when they do something to change? Should you give *them* this book to read? Would your life change as a result? Surely you realize that thinking this way is ludicrous and will guarantee that you live the life of victim versus victor.

Think clearly.

Hold yourself to the highest standards: Step up to full cause at all levels. That means when an earthquake or murder happens in your world, ask yourself, "Why and how did I create this?

What about me needs shaking up?" or possibly "What about me needs to die?"

So are you really ready to walk the path of power? Make the commitment to hold yourself to the highest standard you could ever imagine possible. Refuse to settle for less. Refuse to wallow with the mediocre masses. Always give more than expected, and you will accomplish more than you ever imagined, and you will fully own everything you create.

Realize You Are a Field of Energy

PRINCIPLE THIRTEEN

A T their core, the teachings of all great sages, initiates, and saints since time immemorial share the following. The power to win in life comes from two things:

- You must constantly study, understand, and immerse yourself in that which brings you power; and

- You must avoid at all costs everything that weakens you.

For a life of true and lasting power, it is critical to understand that *everything* counts. Even when you think your action may just be a minor infraction, it counts. Everything counts! The warrior has the ability to impeccably stalk all of his or her weaknesses, in all areas.

I trust it is self-evident that thus far we have been discussing the principles you must consistently study, immerse yourself in, and understand. These principles and all that follows will bring you tremendous power when, and if, you move them from intellectual understandings into physical/spiritual practices.

Just as important, you must avoid energies that weaken you physically, emotionally, mentally, and spiritually. The impeccable warrior realizes that everything counts and will not be satisfied until all lower-level energies are eradicated. Low-energy foods and drinks that rob you of vitality must go; energy vampires, negative relationships and destructive environments must change; thoughts of limitation, self-deprecation, and lack must be removed. As you are surely now fully aware, the path of power is a warrior's path, and it will never be crowded; most often, it will also be difficult.

Truly, everything in your life is either an energy expense or an energy income. Therefore, if you constantly allow your thoughts, habits, and actions to take energy from your reserves, you will never have the opportunity to escalate your power. The ancient Kahuna were really attuned to even the slightest flux in their energy. If they ate or drank something and arose the next morning feeling "off the mark," they would remove the culprit immediately from their lives. The practice of "Ho'o mana" (meaning to make life energy or power) was strictly practiced.

Consistently, I experience would-be warriors coming to a JOURNEY OF POWER event, immersing themselves in high levels of consciousness and energy, only to return to an environment, diet, relationship, or thought pattern of toxic waste. For this reason, many spend their lives on a power roller coaster–up then down, strong then weak, happy then sad, loving then hateful.

The sage is consistently in pursuit of impeccability in all areas of life, realizing that everything counts.

The physical vehicle you ride in is a field of energy; therefore, clean up your body. Imagine investing in a million-dollar racehorse, starving it one day, then feeding it junk foods like candy bars and potato chips, exercising it inconsistently, then expecting it to win the Kentucky Derby. You would not do this. And yet, isn't your physical body worth at least as much attention as a racehorse? Or a fine car? Or your home? This is not a book on nutrition–there are plenty out there. But I guarantee you will never scale the mountains of power with a weak body. And you won't do it carrying a lot of excess baggage.

Clean up your mind.

Your thoughts are creative impulses of energy and information. This can be readily measured by the science of today. Therefore, guard this most powerful energy closely. If your friends spoke to you the way you often speak to yourself, would they be your friends? Unfortunately, the answer is frequently an emphatic no. I have some of my students write down every single thought they have (and can capture) during a four-hour period of one day. They are often shocked and surprised. (It's hard to argue with the written truth.)

Toxic thoughts of fear, anger, regret, self-doubt, hatred, jealousy, and self-deprecation are poisonous to your system. You know this is true, and you also know that to be a warrior you must avoid that which weakens your mind. So clean it up!

Clean up the energy field of your environment. Messy and chaotic environments are the product of a lazy ego waiting for mommy to pick up everything. Remove visual noise and toxic waste from your home, office, and surroundings. Clean out those old clothes that you will never wear again–what are you attached to? Let them go. They are crowding your space. Remember, you are not your things.

Can you sit for one hour in total silence in your own home? Could you do it for a whole day?

Most environments are full of noise and distraction. Most wet-paper-baggers have to immediately turn on some music, news, or a television program. These are all addictions of the ego, which does not want you to find your true self. Power manifests in the energy field of silence and solitude.

Do you like yourself enough to be totally alone and silent in your own company?

Avoid weakness–clean up your environment.

Clean up the energy field of your relationships. One of the most frequently asked questions I receive when speaking of energy vampires is, "James, you tell us to avoid vampires... what if I am sleeping with a vampire?"

Couples who do not grow together will not stay together. Everyone has the choice to either leave and continue the journey, or halt the journey and remain stuck. It's a tough choice, and I am not here to make it for you.

If you think you can change your partner into someone different, I have three words for you: "Get over it!" You can have an influence on another person, but you know you can never change them–you can only change yourself.

So if you are "sleeping with the vampire," first realize that this is only your perspective, not the only possible truth. Try asking your partner if he or she is willing to grow with you, to change the energy-exchange patterns in the relationship that don't support both of you in becoming more. If the person says no, he or she isn't interested in growth, not yours or anyone else's, then you have a pretty clear picture of where this person stands on the spiritual spectrum. Now you have a choice to make.

Even when we go beyond romantic relationships, the same principle holds true. One of the most difficult (and most powerful) choices I ever made was to leave a group of good friends who were not going in the same direction I was. I recognized that they were great people, but for me to spend large quantities of time with them was toxic and holding me back. You will never increase your energy and power by constantly weakening yourself and draining your resources.

What relationships do you currently have that are long overdue to be cleaned up or let go? As you expand and grow, you absolutely must change your inner circle of friends and confidantes. When people's opinions of you are based on who you used to be, those people can keep you stuck. Avoid vampires.

- Do you listen to the scuttlebutt, gossip, and negative comments about others?

- Are you often the instigator of such comments?

You know these types of conversations are not propagating goodness and power and are not meant to help. They are meant to hurt and harm–and the greatest hurt and harm is gifted right back to you. What you put out is what you will get back.

Propagators of this type of negative energy are extremely insecure, attempting to prove to themselves and others that they are better than they feel inside. Love them, understand them, but avoid them–and by all means, don't be one of them.

If you are constantly surrounding and immersing yourself in weakening energies, you will be weak, plain and simple. You may be disciplined in your study of and immersion in powerful energy fields at this point in your journey. However, if you are consistently off-setting this power by allowing equally weakening energies in your field, you will be in equilibrium at best, and you will regress at worst.

In my JOURNEY OF POWER live events, I introduce warriors to a methodology that allows them–beyond question–to know what has the ability to strengthen and what weakens. But until the time we meet face-to-face, avoid those things you intuitively know to be weakening.

Remember, the only reason you are here is to expand your consciousness. Begin to view all life's actions as an exchange of energy. Notice how everything increases or decreases your vitality and power. Realize that you are a field of energy operating and interacting with other fields.

Life gives exams and until you pass, you must take them over and over again. Expedite the process by consistently immersing yourself in power and, just as important, avoid all that weakens.

Just a reminder–the path of power is a warrior's path... and it will never be crowded. This practice will not be the path of the masses, but the gifts, the wonder, the fulfillment, and the joy that it brings is ineffable.

Use Your Body as a Tool of Power

Principle Fourteen

We have already covered many issues pertaining to this principle:

- You are more than a physical being.

- Even though you are a spiritual being, you are here to experience the physical, not to renounce the physical.

- You must avoid, in all areas, that which weakens.

- You will never scale the mountain of power with excess baggage (also known as "extra weight").

Living a life of power is the increased ability to collect, condense, and escalate your energy (CCE). You will experience the ability to CCE when your entire being is firing all cylinders: the body is flexible and strong, the mind is focused on the positive, the spirit is connected to the divine.

The warrior is the person who possesses true power. As we discussed previously, this is not some "foo-foo, wishy-washy, step into the light and rub my crystal" type of approach, but the ability to do things that most mere mortals would call miracles.

All great sages, initiates, and teachers have told us that anything they did, we can do.

With this in mind, consider if the enlightened Christ was overweight and weak. No way. Jesus is believed to have been a student of the Essene tradition, as well as others. This great brotherhood is well-documented to have stringent physical labor as part of its tradition. He was most probably strong as an ox and extremely fit.

Conversely, attend any religious gathering today, and you will find few people with ox-like strength (a backside as big as an ox, maybe, but with the strength of an ox, not so many).

By now you should be well aware that the life of power is a spiritual journey. The question may be, "What do my physical strength and fitness have to do with spiritual power, James?" Answer: Everything!

The weakest link in the chain will either harm you or imprison you. As you begin to move greater levels of energy through your circuits, you will literally be transforming at the cellular level. Sound mystical? It is.

Your body is the conduit through which you flow energy. If that conduit is not strong, you will blow a circuit. Whatever you don't address now will show up in later days in uglier ways.

What's more, if you don't take care of the body, where you are grounded to physical reality, you can "space out." Have you ever met someone who is so far out there that they no longer function in consensual reality? Boy, I sure have!

Being unique is commendable, but if you cannot channel your power into something productive and actually create results in the consensual world, you are not fulfilling your purpose.

I have found diet to be key in keeping myself grounded.

Vegetarianism did not benefit me when I began doing tremendous energy work. I was a pure vegetarian for five years, and when I started visiting the realms of higher consciousness, my insulin levels went wild. Unless you want to live your life in space, you'll need good solid proteins to help keep you grounded.

Be disciplined enough to "eat to live" and not "live to eat."

Eating junk food and allowing yourself to be overweight are the products of a lazy ego lacking discipline. Take charge, warrior–eat for power!

You must also discern the difference between health and fitness. We live in a world fixated on fitness but focused very little on health, concentrated on the cosmetics of appearance instead of on the core vitality of a person.

Doesn't it make more sense to study the cause of what you want (health) instead of the cause of what you don't want (disease)?

Despite its intentions to the contrary, the medical community in many ways fosters illness by making disease its focus of study. Many physicians know far more about disease processes than about prevention or about optimizing good health.

I am sure the drug companies and economic pressures in the medical industry have nothing to do with this one! Yeah, right!

You will not walk the path of power if you look good on the outside, but your internal picture is bleak. Imagine the person who continually washes and waxes the car, but never changes the oil. Many beautiful bodies may be long overdue for an internal clean-up and/or tune-up. Focus on heath and let fitness be the by-product.

You have been given muscles for a reason–use them. The muscle that is not exercised on a regular basis (a minimum of three times a week), begins to atrophy and die. Prepare in advance: As your energy grows, you will be taxing your body at greater and greater levels.

Your muscles do two things: contract and stretch. Contraction comes from heavy, intense yet brief exercise. Stretching is slow, steady exercise, and is equally important.

A lack of flexibility was my downfall for many years. After a long history of weightlifting with no stretching, I began to have physical problems. Contracting my muscles and pushing myself to the limit for over a decade left my body rigid and locked. Energy backed up in my lower body and my shoulders. Yoga was my solution; getting past the tight hamstrings and knots in my shoulders came fairly quickly, and the benefits were enormous. Flexibility and suppleness are life; rigidity is death. An inflexible body indicates an inflexible mind–as within, so without.

Rigid and locked muscles are poor energy conduits. Great amounts of energy are able to rush through your body, but energy cannot go where it cannot flow.

Your body is an intelligent mechanism–pain is its signal to you that something is wrong. We live in a culture that wants to suppress pain, rarely wanting to listen to any message being communicated.

When your back is hurting, it is not time to take an aspirin or to slap on some quick-fix cream–it is time to listen to the signal. Remember to be at cause, and address the cause instead of the effect. Make physical aches and pains your friends by realizing they are letting you know that something is out of order.

If you truly are on the warrior's path, build a powerful, healthy, and flexible conduit now–before pain has to show you your weak links. You will be glad you did.

Rest is as vital as exercise.

There is a time to act and a time to regroup, and you must know when the time is right for each. If you are constantly going and going, you will eventually break.

Imagine pulling onto the highway in a high-performance car, accelerating up to about eighty miles per hour for mile after mile. Eventually, you will have to pull off the highway and refuel. There is no choice involved–even if you fool yourself into believing you can go on indefinitely, you cannot.

The warrior values his dream time as highly as his time awake. Powerful work is done in both realms. One of the greatest ways to access the second ring of power discussed earlier is through practices in dream time, such as lucid dreaming (being consciously aware during dreams).

The life of power incorporates plenty of rest and sleep without overdoing it–you know the difference. And never use sleep as an escape mechanism. Your sly and wily ego produces this strategy when it is afraid to face challenges and opportunities for growth. Situations that are not faced show up physically and psychologically at a later date–often at an inconvenient time. (Remember, life gives exams: If you don't pass them, you must take them over and over until you do.)

Rest, relax, but never allow yourself to get soft.

The life of power incorporates a healthy diet, exercise for muscle strength and tone, flexibility, rest, and relaxation: the complete and total preparation physically, mentally, and spiritually to escalate energy. Prepare yourself to raise the amps, warrior–use your body as a tool of power.

Just Be

HAVE you ever thought about the fact that you are called a human being? Why not a human *doing*? There is a reason.

The ego is a doing entity, and as you now know, it is rare that anyone in our society can even answer a question regarding who they are without utilizing something that they *do* as an answer.

Studying any great tradition, you will find that without exception, there are only two ways the candidate can reach a state of enlightenment:

· Rites of passage

· Individual silence

We could discuss the necessity of rites of passage for some time and maybe never reach a definitive answer. My experience is that it is not the ritual that brings power to you; it is what you bring to the ritual. Ultimately, rituals are unnecessary, as they are not the path to power; they point to the path.

I have been a participant in many rites and rituals, and for me they have all been profound. However, on some occasions when I have had an epiphany, there have been others participating with me who received nothing. It is not what you do; it is how you do it.

The Essenes, Druids, Christians, Jewish mystics, and all shamans have these rites of passage to a higher realm. For me, the rites and initiations I have experienced have been profound in my advancement and understanding–because I intended them to be so.

While the journey of power affords you the opportunity for many rites, experiences, and adventures, they are of no avail in and of themselves. Your intention determines the outcome.

Silence, stopping the world, what many have called meditation, on the other hand, is a different story. Often I hear individuals say, "Well, I tried meditation, but it just doesn't work for me." This is like saying, "Weight-lifting doesn't work on my muscles," which is equally ludicrous.

While you may be able to advance your consciousness without ritual and rites, I guarantee you will not stand a chance without a regular, consistent time of silence.

You must take time to be: You must take time to reconnect with the ocean of consciousness from which you were born and to which you will return. And interestingly enough, this may be one of the most foreign practices with which you must become familiar.

Power manifests in silence. Noise (your ego's first love), on the other hand, is diffused power.

I recall attending a three-day silent retreat some years ago. While I was geared and ready for my three-day internal journey, I found many of the other attendees unwilling; some found it impossible.

I was assigned two roommates who broke silence within an hour after it began. I found myself moving from table to table in the dining room as conversations consistently broke out around me. Since life always provides us exactly what we need, even though I did not get the silence I desired, I had the opportunity to work on my patience and non-attachment.

> The ego is a doing, having, talking, activity-
> craving entity.

Walk into the average home and you will find very little silence. It would aggravate the average individual no end to sit in silence with eyes closed for ten minutes, much less an hour! But the initiate must do what others won't.

Our society as a whole does not support a regular practice of stopping the internal dialogue–nor does traditional Western religion. Most of our silent time is spent "talking to" God. Talk, talk, talk: "God give me this, God give me that, God get me the hell outta this mess that I have created! If you do, I promise to be better in the future."

This stems from the childish view that God is some big daddy in the sky who is going to bless us and save us if we are good enough. This tradition of begging, pleading, and abiding by the rules was invented solely by the limited human mind in an attempt to define what it did not understand.

When you stop talking and start listening, your energy begins to increase–you step into the realms of Spirit and higher consciousness and truly experience real power for the first time.

I promise that when you begin the practice of stopping the world and stepping into the second ring of power, the ego will fight you every step of the way. It will make your nose itch, it will make you physically uncomfortable, it will tell you that you need to get going, it will remind you of all the activities you need to complete today, and it will tell you how stupid you are to be sitting here "doing nothing" when you have so much to do.

You must have the courage and discipline to experience these distractions and persevere anyway.

As you develop the ability to quiet your mind, you also discipline your ego–you take back your power and put your higher self in the driver's seat, usurping the small ego-self. As we have previously discussed, this is exactly what the ego fears most, for this is the death of its power and hold over you.

To find out where you are in the practice of "being" in a space of non-doing, look at these four levels of meditation, each one more powerful than the next:

1. **Visualizing.** This is the entry level of going inside and shutting off the external senses. Sight is a physiological phenomenon–seeing physical data with the eyes. Vision, on the other hand, is a spiritual phenomenon–seeing an internal potential and possibility.

   When you visualize, you design your spiritual prototype. When you imprint it powerfully on the screen of your mind, you literally broadcast energetic vibrations that set in motion an attractive power to manifest what you choose to create in your life. It is not the purpose of this writing to dive deeply into manifestation technologies, as I have discussed this topic in previous books and learning systems.

   Much of what we have been conditioned to believe is prayer is nothing more than noise on your knees. True prayer is imprinting your intention clearly onto your unconscious mind and projecting it into higher conscious mind.

   While visualizing is powerful for manifesting on the physical plane, it is still a form of doing. There are greater levels still of truly "being."

2. **Listening.** Your intuition is your higher self speaking to you, and it is never wrong. The ability to tap into your higher conscious self will take practice and discipline, but the reward is well worth the investment.

   As you transcend your ego chatter, you will begin to experience feelings and messages. It stands to reason that you will never hear the messages being broadcast if you are not quiet long enough to listen.

3. **Static Transcendence.** As power and consciousness increase, you begin to tap into the unmanifest... total awareness... the ineffable. This field of all possibility is pre-form and pre-thought. As you travel into this realm, you move into higher and higher energy fields, and at this point, even the messages you once received will cease. This is a place that is impossible to explain to someone who hasn't been there. This energy field is pre-form yet allness, pre-thought yet limitless. Once you experience it, you will know.

4. **Mobile Transcendence.** After exploring the realms of the ineffable for a time, your next adventure will be to transfer this same state of power into your day-to-day life. You can measure your level of consciousness by the gap that exists between observation and judgment. In other words, when your senses register a physical phenomenon, how long does it take for you to form a judgment (thought) about that phenomenon? The longer it takes you to formulate your opinion, the greater the transcendence and level of consciousness.

This is difficult, as you may imagine. Mobile transcendence begins with stepping into the higher conscious realms with eyes closed (static transcendence) and, once fully anchored there, opening your eyes and seeing how long you can stay in that place. Once you have experienced this, you begin to layer and build; adding movement, walking, talking, and day-to-day activities. The ultimate objective is to cultivate the ability to "just be" (versus thinking, having, and doing) at will. This is the highest state attained by the sage.

So where do you begin? Wherever you are currently with this practice, start with a few minutes a day, three times per week, with an ultimate goal of working toward a daily practice of at least fifteen minutes. As a first step, while you're reading this book, become aware of your feet on the floor. Put your attention on your ankles, your calves, your thighs. Attend to each body part for a few seconds, until you reach the top of your head and the ends of your hair. (Meditation is not just sitting in a lotus position and chanting "om.")

Next, set aside some time to be alone. Sit erect, either with your legs crossed in front of you or in a comfortable chair. Close your eyes and attend to your breath. Breathe in deeply and out slowly. Feel your abdomen rise and fall. If thoughts intrude, let them pass without exploring them. (I think it was Marianne Williamson who suggested you say to yourself, "Thank you for sharing," which I've found to be a useful way to acknowledge while dismissing the thought.)

That's a start. There are many ways to stop the world; find one that works for you. The important thing is, if you ever hope of reaching the fullness of your identity and potential, you must begin and, more important, continue.

Stop the World

PRINCIPLE SIXTEEN

THERE are three temporal locations in which you can live: past, present, and future. All are illusion save one.

There is really only one true answer to the questions "Where are you?" and "What time is it?" You are here and the time is now. All other answers are just fabrications of the mind.

Interestingly enough, here and now are the states of being the ego most resists. To be in the present means the ego has to let go of its attachments and, in effect, die.

You have already read about the necessity of erasing your personal history, yet many of us live a major portion of our lives in the past. Regretting a path not taken, hanging on to the good old days, or being emotionally attached to the way things used to be are all thieves of power and a waste of energy. The past is the past, and it exists only in your mind. All you can do with it is learn from it, apply the learning, and move forward. Let the dead bury the dead!

Likewise, many people live their lives in the future. The ego's incessant desire to have more/do more makes the future attractive. The mind that focuses on "When I get this," "When I accomplish that" disallows the individual the ability to appreciate what is currently happening in life–another thief of power.

Imagine your thoughts as streams of energy: Your ability to collect, condense, and escalate energy determines your level of power. It stands to reason that if you are constantly shooting streams of energy into the past with memories, attachments, regrets, and longings, or constantly shooting streams of energy into the future with wants, goals, wishes, and desires, you will have less energy to give to the present.

As obviously destructive as this cycle may seem, this is how most people live their lives.

Do you agree that the issues of the past are set in stone, and any attempt to chip away at them is futile? You must get over it–stop blaming mommy and daddy–stop reminiscing and yearning.

The future is pure potential and exists only in your imagination. So many people save all their money for rainy days or retirement, that grand pay-off in the future, only to live with very few experiences, ending up old, alone, and full of lost opportunities.

Get over it–stop wishing, desiring, and promising that something will be different when this or that happens. Be here now! Give up the small ego definition of "what should be" and just experience and celebrate what is. Stop the world of ego memory and imagination, and step into the second ring of power that exists only and always in the present moment.

You must pre-live the future, not relive the past, and savor the moment.

Pre-living the future is not constantly projecting energy into the formless void. It is the process of setting a clear intention. Much like taking a trip, you must clearly know where you are going before you begin. Likewise, you must set an intention, specifically defined, and visualize it clearly–the first step of meditation discussed previously. The key is to then let it go and focus on the current moment.

Think of it this way: If you were to drive from San Diego to Atlanta, you would first look at the map, find your destination, and then decide on your route. Once in the car you don't continue to look for Atlanta; you look at the road immediately in front of you. If you continue to look at the map or into the far-off distance, you will miss the highways and turns you need to make, not to mention the scenery. You have to be focused in the present–looking at the road in front of you. Stop the world of imagining and start living!

When you stop reliving the past, you understand that the issues of the past are set in concrete: Any attempt to chip away at them or change them is futile. You could erase your history in an instant if you would only do it. In my QUANTUM LEAP event, we use a methodology that quickly and elegantly releases limiting beliefs, decisions, and emotions from your unconscious mind. This is effective yet so simple that if you decide to do this for yourself, you absolutely can. Stepping into your full power is a process of re-membering your divinity. Stop the world of memory–intend it, decide it, and walk into a new future.

The great paradox is that the only way you can step into a new future is through the gateway of the present. The warrior understands that he will never escalate his power to the level necessary to escape the collective consciousness (what I call escape velocity) until he can generate enough energy into the present moment.

Obviously the meditation techniques in Principle 15 are the cornerstone to your success in stopping the world. If you can imagine that every single thought is an impulse of energy, and that like energies are attracted to each other, then you can imagine the strength contained in the energy field of socially conditioned thought. Imagine each similar thought, of each similar fashion, collecting together in the energy field of earth. Think how attractive and powerful that field must be! You probably realize it would take an enormous amount of energy for you to reach escape velocity from this matrix. Luckily, a committed group of misfit and maverick free-thinkers are rapidly reducing the gravitational pull. The spiritual radicals of our planet are consistently putting out vibrations of a higher order and, once critical mass is reached, we will leap to a new level. This leap is known in the world of quantum physics as a "phase transition."

A phase transition phenomenon is observed by physicists when aligning quantum particles. When a critical number (critical mass) of quantum particles are aligned in the same direction, *all other particles* immediately fall into alignment. We are living in an age in which critical mass is being accumulated in the consciousness of mankind. As this mass continues to build, there will come a time when we will collectively and rapidly leap to a new level of awareness and being.

Once your regular practice of stopping the world is in place, the next thing you can do to center yourself in the present (versus past or future) is to constantly notice the sensations in your body. For instance, while I am writing this, I am feeling the chair underneath me (a nice cushy leather high-back), my feet on the floor, and I am totally focused on the one thing in which I am involved, which is writing.

I am not thinking about the next principle I'll write, the last, or what I am going to do tomorrow–I am fully present in the writing of this material. Because this book has been written with this type of presence and energy, the very reading of it can assist you in the escalation of your consciousness. I encourage you to read it again and again–in fact, don't just read it, study it.

In my JOURNEY OF POWER events I always have at least one opportunity that I call a "radical spiritual experience," which intensely brings people into the present moment, because that's where God Spirit resides. The warriors who have joined me have accomplished and experienced things you may not be able to imagine. The value of these radical experiences is not in the often-experienced adrenaline rush or in breaking fear barriers, but in the experience of being totally present in the now.

When you are stretching beyond your comfort zone physically, spiritually, and emotionally, you are totally present. The best example I can give you is to reflect upon a time when you have been in a challenging situation. I guarantee you were not worried about your future bills when you were about to rear-end someone in traffic, or were hanging off a cliff by your fingertips-you were totally and completely focused on the task at hand!

A radical spiritual experience includes anything that facilitates your focus on the present moment. Once you know how to travel to a new level of power, your chances of getting back to that place are greatly enhanced.

Starting today, begin to discipline your unruly mind-stop the world.

When you are reading, read; when you are writing, write; when you are eating, eat; when you are walking, walk. See how present you can be in whatever you are doing. Rather than doing ten things at once, do one thing fully and completely. This does not mean you have to slow down your pace-in fact, you will find that you get so much more accomplished. More important, you will get so much more out of life.

I guarantee you will find this challenging at first, but with persistence you will find your power escalating. And believe me, there will be interruptions, either physically or psychologically, that you cannot avoid. Deal with the physical interruptions, then get right back to your focus. Acknowledge the psychological interruptions (thoughts), then return to your focus.

Resolve to stay out of the illusion of past and future. Step into your power-be here now, my radical warrior friend.

Follow Your Intuition

PRINCIPLE SEVENTEEN

YOUR intuition is your higher self speaking to you—and your higher self knows all. To access this unlimited power source on a continuing basis, it is necessary to understand something about how consciousness works.

There are five levels of consciousness, but we will review only three right now: unconscious mind (UCM), conscious mind (CM), and higher conscious mind (HCM). They all are equally important, yet very different.

Your UCM is the emotional mind, running your entire body without the ability to think or reason. It is a stimulus/response entity. Your UCM houses all your experiences and suppresses the ones you choose not to deal with at any given time. The clearer this part of your mind, the more powerful conduit of communication it will be. (In other words, the most powerful practice available for your UCM is to eradicate limiting beliefs, decisions, and emotions from your consciousness.) This part of you is very important in that HCM/intuition communicates to you through your UCM in dreams, metaphors, and feelings.

When there are tremendous blocks and barricades in your UCM, the messages of HCM will never make it through—yet another reason why erasing your past is a vital focus for the warrior.

The CM is the part of you that thinks and reasons, and it is both a blessing and a curse. It is a blessing in that it gives you the ability to choose how you will think and what you will create in your life. It is a curse in that your CM is the domain of the ego and therefore can become your nemesis, blocking your access to your spiritual nature. You cannot think your way to God Spirit–you can only *experience* God Spirit.

You must shut down the intellectual ego, with all of its petty thoughts, wishes, desires, and wimpy, whiny ways, in order to access your complete self by plugging into full, transcendent power.

HCM is actually your higher self: the God Spirit living in and through you. It will never impose its ways upon you–it will never override the CM and its ego/intellect–but it is always ready, willing, and able when invited. The answer to every question in every situation resides in HCM. To tap into this limitless inventory of power, you must do a few things...

1. **Get your ego/intellect out of the way.** Many of the things that will bring you the greatest power and greatest return will appear crazy to the analytical mind–and to most of your friends. That is why you must commit to the life of a warrior. Get your ego out of the way and be willing to let go and flow.

2. **Create a great rapport and communication link between your CM and your UCM.** UCM receives the messages from HCM, and hands them over to your CM through your intuitive factor. You must learn to listen to what is being communicated.

3. **Forget information–pursue experience.** At the level of HCM, there is no substitution for direct personal experience. When you are operating "in spirit," you are inspired. When you are stuck "in form," you want loads of in-formation. Study is powerful and useful to gaining speed and

power, but ultimately you must move beyond study to personally *experience* your higher self.

Once you have stepped into the realm of the gods, no one and no-thing can tell you any different–you just know!

It is critical to make a distinction between emotions and feelings. Emotions are reactionary and about as predictable as a wild boar. Those who live a life based on emotions are on a constant roller-coaster ride that is neither productive nor fun to be around. You probably know someone like that.

Feelings, on the other hand, are messages from HCM.

It is difficult to explain and/or define this messenger–it is something that must be experienced. Feelings may come to you in the form of a vision, a gut-level vibration, an internal auditory statement or a host of other sensations. Often I have been asked, "How do you know the difference? How can you tell?"

Because this is experiential knowledge, the only answer I can give is that it takes practice and intention to tell the difference; it cannot be taught.

I began discriminating between emotions and feelings years ago. When I got an internal message of any sort I would respond–even if it seemed silly. If I got great results, I thought, "Bingo! Intuition." If it did not work out too well, I knew it was emotion. With every success I experienced I inventoried exactly what happened to me internally and externally. Finally I began to know the difference–and you will, too.

Once you cleanse your UCM of unwanted blockages, build a loving relationship and rapport between your CM and UCM, and avidly pursue personal experience, then you will be plugged into the All-Knowing.

Here are a couple of insights from this realm.

First, you can't push the stream. Even though I write and teach these things, sometimes even I need to be reminded.

Second, know when to act. Just as important, know when not to act.

For years I have studied and learned how energy works and how to manifest results into physical form. A few years back I wrote a book entitled *The Science of Success*, which discussed these topics, and I was flying high.

Using my manifestation abilities, I had accumulated quite a large amount of things: a big house, big mortgage, expensive cars, fine clothes–you get the picture.

Well, upon the dissolution of a personal relationship, I conducted a personal inventory and decided to live the life of a warrior. I determined that freedom and flexibility and being lean and mean were the way to go. I released myself of the bricks and mortar (and mortgage) and pared down. Less was more.

This was great for a little over two years. I was single, my focus was solely on the expansion of my own consciousness, I was traveling to study with my teachers–I was escalating and feeling powerful. Guess what? Spirit decided it was time for a test.

I got into a relationship with a fine young lady and, getting all caught up in the romance of things, forgot my earlier commitment. Isn't it interesting how easily affairs of the heart can do things like that?

Anyway, I decided it was time to get domestic again. Business was good, and I started looking for a house to buy. The signs that this was just not right were there from the start. I began by committing to a much lower price range, which allowed me to justify to myself that I was not "breaking my vow." However, that price started inching up little by little with every outing. If you have ever purchased a house you know how easily the real-estate agent and the ever-thirsty ego can jump your financial commitment dramatically. I found a home I liked and made an offer on it, and it was declined without a counter. I found a second home and was the second offer in line; the seller took the first offer. Did

I pay attention? No way. I continued to push upstream! I found a third house, and this time my offer was the third simultaneous offer in a hot market–the seller took the second offer.

By this time, I should have stepped back and listened. One of my teachers told me, "You can never push the stream, James. You must flow with the stream." Instead of flowing, my ego convinced me that this was just a test of my willingness to stick with it and hang in there. We are rationalizing beings, which is most often nothing more than rationing-lies to ourselves.

I hung in there and continued my search. Finding a fourth home, I put in an offer and it was accepted. Success at last! However, the appraisal came in way below the offered price. I did not feel good about this at all but by this time I was already in motion and emotionally committed. The realtor got busy getting different "comps" so as to substantiate the loan.

At this point, Spirit had given me no less than five solid signals that this was not to be my path. You would think I would listen–what does it take? The next wake-up call was a sledge-hammer between the eyebrows!

A few days before closing, I found that tens of thousands of dollars had been embezzled from my business, and terrible misinformation was found in my bookkeeping. Bottom line: The monies I thought were available were not.

This final smack in the face woke me up, and I pulled out of escrow. Not, by the way, without losing a large chunk of change that I had put down as earnest money.

Lesson learned again–the hard way. You cannot push the stream.

Once again I realized that I had been caught up in an ego acquisition mode that really was not part of my path at that time. Spirit had other plans. Listen to your higher self, and you will not make the same errors over and over.

If something feels right, then take action–even if all logic seems to tell you otherwise. Just make sure it is a *feeling*, not an ego desire or emotionally driven action.

If it doesn't feel right, then don't act–wait. Waiting is often just as powerful as action. Just make sure it is not procrastination or fear causing you to pause.

As you begin to practice following your intuition, you will become stronger and more powerful. The secret is just to constantly listen and follow the message.

The ego and social consciousness are formidable opponents. These two forces will use everything in their power to hold you back and keep your true self at bay. The path of power is the warrior's path... and it will never be crowded!

Stand "For" Instead of "Against"

PRINCIPLE EIGHTEEN

DURING the Vietnam War, Mother Teresa was asked, "Will you march with us to protest the war?" She calmly replied, "No, but when you have a march for peace, I will be there."

Anything you resist persists—you give life to anything you fight. Love flows where attention goes. Taking a strong stand against anything is a dysfunctional type of love that continues to feed the monster.

I recall a situation in which an ex-employee was quite upset with me. This person felt he had been wronged and was determined to let everyone possible know: my clients, my prospects, my current employees, anyone and everyone within earshot. I never responded.

Many of my close friends and associates commented, "You have to do something about this! How about suing him?" Some of them even got angry on my behalf. Much to their dismay, I did nothing, and as a result I accomplished everything. The warrior knows when to act and when to wait.

I realized that no one with any power would buy into this nonsense anyway. Like attracts like, and anyone who would listen had to be in a similar mental space as this person. My lack of concern and attention caused the situation to dry up and blow away.

What did Jesus mean when he said, "Resist not evil"? Evil is illusion: If you check the root of the word evil, it comes from Greek, meaning "to veil or hide." Evil is nothing more than a veil that hides the truth of all goodness, and it has no power unless given energy from you.

A Course in Miracles states, "If you defend yourself, you are attacked." Nothing real can be threatened; only illusion can be threatened. Reality is changeless and eternal: everything else comes and goes.

When you take a stand against something, you are defending a foundation of sand and giving energy to "evil."

A "war on terrorism" gives energy and life to the very thing it is claiming to end. There is a time and a place for movements and for doing good, but as you evolve you will find your attraction to these "causes" lessening and lessening. *A Course in Miracles* also states, "All things are echoes of the voice of God."

As the warrior continues to scale the mountain of consciousness, he or she lets go of "fix-it" causes and recognizes that *everything* is perfect and divine. Everything happens for a reason, and everything is exactly as it should be according to the grander plan.

If you rant and rave against politicians and social issues, you don't get it. This approach is the ego's attempt to prove that it knows how things "should be." This is the utmost in arrogance, for what you are really saying is that you should be in charge, not Spirit. Evolution is a process.

> The current state of affairs is a direct reflection
> of the consciousness level of mankind.

Advance the consciousness, and the effects have no choice but to follow. Also realize that for anything new to live, something first must die—and death is never easy.

Chaos theory tells us that apparent chaos, from a higher perspective, is actually extremely organized. Often we just don't have the ability to rise high enough above the situation to see the broader view. A life of power contains the ability to see the big picture, to take life as it comes, realizing that all is in perfect order no matter how chaotic it may seem.

Does this mean you should not attempt to improve things? Not at all. But the most efficient way to improve the world is to escalate your own power. Jesus said, "If I be lifted up, I lift up every man."

Every advance you make in your own energy, consciousness, and power is an advance for the entire human race. The greatest good you can do, the greatest gift you can give, is the advancement of your self. Talk about impact: Walking the path of power is advancing the human race now and in the future.

If you feel compelled to act on something, make certain you are acting to create something, not acting to eradicate something. Stand for instead of against. This is a fine distinction, but the mind cannot process a negative. In other words, if I tell you, "Don't think about war," what do you have to think about to make sense of the sentence? You have to think about what not to think about.

What you focus on, you create and attract. Your focus is your point of love.

Make your primary focus the escalation of your consciousness. Constantly collect, condense, and escalate your energy. The greatest way to do this is to consistently focus on what you *choose* versus what you don't want, what you stand *for* instead of against. In this way you utilize your energy most powerfully and give life to your advancement versus retreat.

Just Do
PRINCIPLE NINETEEN

In the East, there is a saying, "Before enlightenment, carry water and sweep floors. After enlightenment, carry water and sweep floors." The point is that what you "do" (your activities) changes very little as your consciousness expands and escalates.

The life of power looks much like any other life from outward appearances. If you were to follow the spiritual warrior around for a day, you would find her making phone calls, keeping appointments, planning and scheduling, eating and sleeping—activities much like everyone else does. The difference does not lie in the external activities but rather in the internal ones.

It is not what you do that determines your power; it is *how* you do it.

This "how" lies in the internal world of your own mind. Again, you can play the game full-on, without buying in. In other words, you recognize it as a game and, while you are giving your full energy and attention to what you are doing, you are not attached to the outcome. Doing for the sake of doing is the ultimate pleasure and power.

Most individuals are doing to "get" versus doing for the love of what is being done. This is a mindset that states, "I am involved in this activity because it will bring me a large return of some nature."

A few years ago I was the keynote speaker at a large conference. This was a group of home-based-business owners in the
health industry. A young man standing backstage introduced
himself and told me that he had just gotten involved in the business. "Congratulations," I told him, and then asked, "Why did
you get involved?" He promptly replied, "I know people can
make a lot of money in this business!" I smiled and said nothing,
but inside I thought, "You aren't going to make it."

Study after study proves that those who reach the pinnacle of
their potential do not do so in pursuit of the money. Money comes
as a by-product of pursuing your passion with excellence.

The person of power does for the sake of doing. In other
words, be involved in an activity because you enjoy (in-joy) the
activity. If you accomplish a certain outcome, that's great, and if
you don't that's okay, as well; you had fun in the process.

The reality is that any time you have accomplished a particular outcome or goal, it is always time for another. Remember,
the ego is never satisfied. When you reach the goal, you may stop
to celebrate and savor the moment, but invariably it is time to
tackle the next peak.

Any true value you garner will be from the process of getting
there. I guarantee as you look back upon your entire life, it is
the paths you have taken, the challenges you have met, and the
experiences you have had that will give you the most memories
and greatest value. True wealth lies in the journey, not the destination: the doing, not the having or getting.

To live a life of power is to learn to enjoy every single moment
of every single day. This is another way to "be here now" and
thereby keep your power collected and condensed.

Never Let an Old Person Move into Your House

PRINCIPLE TWENTY

WHENEVER I say this from stage, invariably a few people in my audience take offense until they realize what I am really talking about.

The house I am referring to here is the house of your spirit–in other words, your body. You don't grow old; when you stop growing you *get old*. I meet so many people on a regular basis who are just warmed-over dead. They haven't done anything outside their routine for years, and they have no plans to, either. All they are waiting for is a few more nails and the coffin is sealed. Unfortunately, this coffin is of their own making.

If you ever visit the Rock and Roll Hall of Fame, you'll see an inscription in large letters that reads, "If you don't like rock and roll, then you are just too old."

Please understand: I am not advocating the wanna-be teenagers who are way past their prime, wearing clothes from their youth that look ridiculous on them now, still attempting to cruise the bars. I am not referring to the grandpas who wear tights to the gym and dress in baggy pants.

I am talking about keeping oldness from creeping in, about staying out of a rut.

When you find yourself in a rut, you are heading toward death. A rut is nothing more than a grave without the top layer of dirt–just a few more shovels full, and you are outta here!

The person of power keeps adventure and excitement at the top of the list.

I live near the ocean. When a strong storm blows in, the tree that can outlast the storm is the tree that can flex and bend. If a tree is rooted rigidly, it is often pulled right out of the earth. When you allow an old person to move in, you become rigid–just like you do when you die.

Rigidity is a sickness of the ego. The ego's primary objective is to survive: Its greatest fear is death. As a result, it attempts to predict and control, and it fools itself into thinking that this predictability will allow it to succeed and survive.

The irony is that the thing it fears the most is the very thing it creates. Predictability is death, and comfort is a state of non-growth. The very thing the ego thinks will bring it immortality and power is actually the next nail in the coffin.

This principle is true of plants and true of people. Anything that is living is blossoming, unfolding, and blooming, with suppleness and flexibility.

Abraham Maslow stated, "He who is good with a hammer thinks everything is a nail." Figuratively, old means getting good with a hammer. Any time you find yourself thinking you have all the answers to life's questions, you are getting old. Youth is a mindset, and youth is openness. Youth is an adventure and a passion for learning and new experiences.

One of the greatest enemies of power is the illusion of clarity. When you begin to believe you are totally clear on all of life's issues and answers, you are making your bed in a graveyard, with stagnation and death for your bedfellows.

The life of power is lived in a state of curiosity and flexibility. Stay open and alive.

Do Small Things Consistently
PRINCIPLE TWENTY-ONE

S MALL things, done consistently in strategic places, create major impact. You will find that in most every area of your life, it is the small things that make the most difference. Think about your relationships–it is not the great gifts or amazing trips that really matter in the grand scheme, but the small "I love you," the "I am there for you when you need me," the "I believe in you" that matter most.

The same is true in both the personal and business aspects of your life. For this reason, you must commit to pristinely executing the important. Consistently, you will find that the most important long-term issues are rarely the most grandiose or the most urgent. Let's explore some of the small things you as a warrior can commit to accomplishing on a regular basis.

Schedule personal quiet and/or think time each day. While this is one of the best uses of time, you will find it infrequently practiced. The collective masses do not value personal time as a high-priority activity and will not encourage or reinforce it. Consider escalating your power as birthing a new identity within you. Just as a small child does, this new identity needs attention and care, or it will not survive.

As we discussed previously, your personal meditation and contemplation time is the single most important investment you can make in the advancement of your power. My most creative life- and business-building ideas have been gifted to me in my quiet times. My most transcendent adventures into HCM have been in this space as well. Think of it this way: What is the potential return on one flash of inspiration? Immeasurable–so just do it!

Handwrite notes. While this is a very simple activity, do not underestimate its potential power. I have garnered multiple thousands of dollars in business by investing the energy to write one well-timed, handwritten note. Small things done consistently in strategic places create major impact.

You, like most modern humans, are probably inundated each day with email, voice mail, phone calls, and faxes. Very few people in today's fast-paced world invest the time to stop and handwrite a note. Don't get me wrong; there is a time and a place for mechanical mediums, but if you really want to make an impact on those whom you serve, pick up your pen, pick out a card, lick a stamp, and drop a note in the mail.

In high-tech society, high touch is highly valued.

Clean and organize your environment. Feng Shui is the Chinese art of energy management and can be a wonderful aid in deciding how to arrange the tangible things in your life for optimum flow of intangible energy. Yet this, like anything, can be taken to an extreme. I once hired a Feng Shui consultant to come into my home, and he went nuts with all the crystals, rules, and regulations. The environment was starting to dictate my energy flow instead of facilitate it. A lot of the paraphernalia, along with the consultant, got transferred to the sidewalk. (Don't let the door "feng" you on your "shui" out!)

An environment either brings power or toxicity into whatever you are involved with. I remember a former peer telling me, "A messy desk and office is a sign of a busy person." Actually, a messy desk and office is a sign of a messy desk and office. Moreover, it is a sign of a lazy ego. Messy environments are an energy drain–the by-product of an ego waiting for "mommy to pick up after it." There is absolutely no excuse for sloppiness.

You will be much more productive and powerful in a clean and organized environment. You will be much more productive and powerful when *you* are clean and organized. Get the visual distractions and scattered notes out of your world. Tuck in your shirt, stand up straight, and pull in your stomach, warrior. Bring power to all areas.

Always give credit rather than take it. The ego wants to be stroked and recognized. The warrior, being self-referring, wants to *give* strokes and recognition. It is a strange but true paradox in life: The more you give away, the more you have.

The sage Lao Tzu walked the earth five hundred years before Jesus and wrote the *Tao Te Ching*. This great work of spiritual mastery has been my constant companion for years upon years and contains incredible insights to a life of power. In a treatise on leadership, Lao Tzu wrote a statement that I believe speaks for itself:

> **True leaders are hardly known to their followers.**
> **Good leaders are those whom people love and admire;**
> **Poor leaders are those whom people fear and despise;**
> **Great leaders are those whose people say, "We did it ourselves."**

Treat everyone as the most important person in the world. Most actions are made out of habit. Often people fool themselves into believing, "When this or that occurs, then I will begin to (fill-in-the-blank)." For example, "When I make more money, then I will save or give to worthy causes." Or "If I get ahead in my business, then I will spend more time with my family." All of these "when/then" or "if/then" ideas are illusions. They are nothing more than excuses of the ego.

Bottom line: If you don't develop the habit of investing wisely when you have very little money, you won't do it when you have truckloads of money. Habits of behavior now will be habits of behavior later. Unless you change the habit, no amount of situational change will change you.

For this reason, you must develop the habit of treating everyone you meet as if you were meeting God Spirit–because you are. Any wet-paper-bagger can be nice to those who will give them something in return: a good client, someone they are sweet on or fond of, someone who is going to further their cause. But it takes a person of higher awareness and power to see the Christ and Buddha in the scruffy, gruff, and potentially unlovely.

Make it a regular practice to treat the grocery store clerk, the bank teller, the street person, and the guy who cuts you off in traffic as if they were people who could make you a million dollars.

Powerful habits like these will serve you and keep you living a life of power.

Keep a journal. Once again, this is a small activity that will prove to be a powerful practice. I am frequently asked, "Do you write in your journal every day?" and "What do you write in it?"

First, I do not write in it every single day–only when I am inspired to do so or I have an experience I want to ponder.

Second, it is important to make the distinction that I define a journal and a diary differently. While I may write some things of a personal nature in my journal, that is not by any means its primary function, although that is the primary function of a diary.

A personal journal is a place to ponder your life experiences, insights, and learning. When I take a trip to the Andes with my teacher, or go to Hawaii to study with my Kahuna, I record the experiences in my journal so I can reflect upon them later. When I attend a personal development seminar, I record my notes in my journal. I put my flashes of insight and inspiration into my journal. I record the messages received during dream time in my journal. Basically, it is a place to capture anything and everything of importance that is going on in my life.

There is tremendous value in capturing this information for future reference. You may find it powerful to look back upon where you were at a certain point in your life and consciousness, and notice how you have grown. How much of your personal history no longer exists?

There have been countless times when I have found humor in the things that were so important to me (and that I was so concerned about) at one point in my life. When viewing them in retrospect, they seem so silly. This is a good confirmation of growth and a great reminder to continue to practice the escalation of my consciousness by letting go of the wake.

An ocean liner is turned 180 degrees by making small changes in coordinates and locking onto those coordinates over miles and miles. A speedboat turns on a dime. Life is an ocean liner, not a speedboat.

Small practices consistently acted upon garner great results over time. When you are faithful over a little, you will be gifted with a lot.

Forgive and Apologize
PRINCIPLE TWENTY-TWO

No one ever died from a snake's bite. A snake bite is a snake bite: Once the snake's fangs leave your flesh, the bite is over. What kills a person is the poison running through the bloodstream. Remove the venom, and you remove the danger.

I once heard it said that refusing to forgive is like drinking poison and expecting the other person to die. A lack of forgiveness is a venom that continues to surge through your veins. For this reason, forgiveness is the greatest gift one can give to oneself: the greatest act of self-love. The main cause of a lack of forgiveness is a lack of love for self. While this may seem initially crazy, and the ego may tell you the exact opposite, as you ponder this concept you will realize it is the most sane truth imaginable.

For-giving is the greatest gift to self, and unless you can give this to yourself, you will never be able to fully give to others. *A Course in Miracles* states, "Forgiveness is the key to salvation, and forgiveness is your function."

Many of us have been conditioned to believe that we must be forgiven by some great method, ritual, or go-between. We must supplicate a teacher or process that becomes the emissary to God Spirit. This is a bunch of childish baloney. You don't need anyone or anything to forgive or save you–save yourself! You are already forgiven–you just must realize it.

"But, James," you may think, "I have been told that I am a sinner and that I need to be saved." Yes, indeed you are, and you do–but let's make sure we understand what "sin" really means. I am willing to bet it's not as ugly as it has been made to sound.

First, the word *sin* comes from a Greek archery term meaning to "miss the mark." Not such a big deal, is it? You certainly shouldn't be the subject of an eternal barbecue for merely missing the mark! And while we are on the subject of hellfire and brimstone, let's shatter some additional misnomers that have festered into facts.

Jesus told us, "The kingdom of heaven is within," and it certainly is not a condo on a cloud. So doesn't it stand to reason that "hell" should be an internal state as well? The idea of a horned demon basting and browning us for eternity came from the childish minds of those who did not understand–and many still don't. We also *used to* believe that the sun died each night and was reborn in the east, that the world was flat, that the sun circled around the earth, that we had to sacrifice animals to please the gods... the list is endless. We let go of so many of these myths; why have we not let go of these other products of childish consciousness?

It is way past time for us to grow up and wake up. We have made major leaps in technology, and yet our traditional religious beliefs are almost unchanged from the Stone Age.

Let go of the idea that you need (or ever did need) someone to die for you because you merely missed the mark. God Spirit doesn't need sacrifices and never did. The only thing you must sacrifice is the fallacy of separateness. Missing the mark is how we most often learn how to hit the mark.

The word *repent* likewise comes from the Greek, meaning to "have a change of heart." Therefore, all you must do to be "saved" and "born again" is to change your heart. "Sinners repent" in the original Greek means, "Those who have missed the mark have a change of heart."

Give yourself the gift of forgiveness, and you will automatically escalate your energy. Stop the world, and be in the eternal now. Anything needing forgiveness must, by its very nature, be something that is past tense. Therefore, lack of forgiveness for self or others is attachment to the past and stealing your power in the present.

You may experience a few snake bites here and there along the path, but you don't have to carry the poison.

This brings us to the idea of apologizing, or asking for forgiveness. Let's agree up front that we are not discussing the wimpy escape mechanism where we just say "I'm sorry" without sincerity–that really is a "sorry" practice. A true apology must be a sincere recognition of something you would like to do differently next time.

I am familiar with several people who have a very difficult time apologizing. This close cousin to a lack of forgiveness keeps energy stuck in the past, disallowing life to move forward.

Just suppose you were to place an extremely dirty pair of gym socks in a locker, lock it up, and leave them for a year. Coming back one year later and expecting them to have cleaned themselves would be ludicrous.

Just as when you practice forgiveness, when you apologize, you do it for the retrieval and escalation of your own energy and power, not for anyone else involved.

It ultimately does not matter whether the other person accepts your apology or not. While it may feel nice if you are forgiven, you cannot control the response. Once you have done your part, you can collect and condense your energy and move on.

So, warrior, give the gift of forgiveness to yourself first, and then to others. Get the dirty socks out of your locker. These two practices will increase your power and velocity, and they just may be the key to a major awakening.

Collapse the World

PRINCIPLE TWENTY-THREE

MANY of my studies and initiations have been in the shamanic traditions of ancient Hawaii (called Huna) and the Peruvian traditions from Vilcambamba, Cusco, and Machu Picchu. I have tremendous respect for the ancient Hawaiians, and possibly even more for the Inca.

The Inca were an incredibly spiritual people–everything to the Inca was of Spirit. No other civilization, save perhaps the ancient Egyptians, accomplished more in the way of spiritual and physical achievement, and certainly none managed to complete them in the short time span in which the Inca existed.

All ancient traditions teach that the consensual world is a world co-created by the collective attention of human minds. We hold the world together with our collective attention, and when we shift our attention, the world as we know it collapses.

While we could carry on an intellectual conversation on this subject for some time, it probably would accomplish little. On the physical plane of existence, there is no substitution for action. On the level of the unconscious mind, there is no substitution for focus. At the conscious level of cosmology, there is no substitution for understanding. And ultimately, at the level of higher conscious mind, nothing substitutes for experience.

There is a crack between the worlds at each level, and you have the ability (and the right) to step into that abyss. Many seminal thinkers have told us through hallucinogenic research that the hallucinogen does nothing more than collapse the consensual world in which we live. The consensual world, once collapsed, allows the adventurer the ability to explore non-ordinary states of reality.

Non-ordinary states of consciousness are every bit as "real" as our typical beta wave operating state, and once you know how to get to these altered planes of existence, you have a greater likelihood of finding your way back. I personally *experienced* more God Spirit in one shamanic journey than I *learned about* God Spirit in my entire traditional church-going years.

Current surveys tell us that while ninety percent of people surveyed believe in God, fifteen percent or less attest to having a direct personal experience of this creative power. To truly experience God Spirit, you have to be willing to let go. You must be willing to collapse the world. (This does not mean, however, that you must do so through hallucinogens. There are other ways, many of which I teach in my JOURNEY OF POWER workshops.)

One of the main things I love about the shamanic traditions is that the shaman gets his power through direct personal revelation. He does not need to attend a certain college, get a certain degree, and have a certain ordination to grant him spiritual prowess. His spiritual power comes directly from the source.

Most people have traded knowing a lot about God for personal experience of God.

As previously discussed, adventures into higher consciousness cannot be taught; they must be experienced. Attempting to "learn" about God Spirit can be compared to reading the menu in a restaurant. While the menu is a description, it is not *the food*. To taste the food, you must actually eat it.

We cannot explore the experiential aspect of these realities together in this book–that is the purpose of my JOURNEY OF POWER events. But from an intellectual standpoint, you can begin to collapse the world through a different way of thinking and being.

The life of an initiate is a life that does not accept at face value what has been handed down from generation to generation. I ask you to consider how free you really are. If you have read this far in this book, you have probably read something which bumps up against the historically programmed way of thinking. Since you are still here, you are probably somewhat open to considering something that goes against the grain. Congratulations!

You will never live a life of power while thinking and playing with the masses. You must collapse that world. The realms of the spiritual warrior are the realms of non-ordinary reality. Once comfortable with these realms, the tracker of power will begin to shift the shape of what appears to be static. What the masses would call miracles, this warrior sees as a normal way of being.

Once again, this level of power will never be accessed without tremendous dedication and a willingness to pay the price for the prize. Are you willing to die to all that you currently know? Are you willing to be washed out completely–to release your personal history and all your attachments?

Begin by refusing to walk the way of the masses. Refuse to buy into the nonsensical ideas that you are what you do or what you have. Refuse to allow your ego to suck you into endless consumerism and overextension. Collapse that world!

Live a life that is lean and mean. Own nothing, for you recognize that you ultimately don't anyway. Collect nothing, for he who collects much has much to lose, whereas he who collects nothing has nothing to lose.

Be ready to move and change directions at the drop of the hat. You will never be able to do this with a bunch of baggage to shuffle and transport. Hold flexibility and freedom in highest regard.

Stay off the bandwagon of patriotism and nationalism. Both are infantile cults that set one race or belief system up as the best, making all others "lesser" or "wrong." Get rid of your labels of Christian, Jew, Hindu, Buddhist, Latter Day Saints, Baptist, or any of the endless lists of "the right way" to God Spirit. All of these labels are products of the ego attempting to have their own personal god favor them most. If all the major religious beliefs think they are right and everyone else is wrong–no one is right!

You are a traveler, a warrior, a citizen of the universe.

When someone asks, "Are you a Christian?" say yes and know that the true meaning of Christian is to *become* Christ rather than worship an icon. If asked, "Are you a Buddhist?" answer yes, knowing that you are *becoming* Buddha rather than worshiping a God incarnate.

The Hopi Indians predicted: "And 144,000 Light warriors, with their shields balanced, recognizing all paths as leading to one, will come to earth in her time of greatest need and teach the teachers."

As a warrior you recognize that all paths lead to the one final outcome. Collapse the world of the masses and step into the abyss of power.

Travel in Dream Time

PRINCIPLE TWENTY-FOUR

Your higher conscious mind (HCM) communicates with your conscious mind (CM) through your unconscious mind (UCM). For this reason, you must pay particular attention to the messages you receive when the HCM sends messages to you through the UCM during dream time.

There are many theories regarding what actually occurs during our dream state, the time when our conscious mind takes a break. Some believe we actually operate in a different reality or state of consciousness. If you feel that dream time is not important, consider this: dream time occupies approximately one-third of your life.

During thirty-three percent of your physical life, your conscious mind shuts down, yet you are still quite active. Your UCM never sleeps. Often called the "body/mind," the UCM beats the heart, runs the respiratory system, digests food, takes you into journeys of non-ordinary consciousness, and allows you to wake to ordinary consciousness while your CM takes a six- to eight-hour break. That break also includes the reception and transmission of messages from HCM–do you realize just how powerful your UCM is ?

As you begin to study and explore dream time, you will recognize the power contained therein.

First, the messages you receive tell you much regarding what is going on in your life and the direction that your higher self is encouraging you to travel.

It is important to realize that the UCM has no ability to think and/or reason. Therefore *every* message you receive in your dream consciousness is not to be taken literally. HCM is sending instructions and/or insights to you through the UCM via analogy, illustration, and metaphor–not through logic.

Consequently, graphic or potentially frightening dreams do not necessarily mean anything bad. My experience with these types of messages reveals that HCM has typically sent me several messages of a similar slant, but with less emotional impact, and I have typically not paid attention. The solution for HCM is to send a message with a greater jolt to get my attention–and it typically works. This may be the case with your bad dreams as well: You *absolutely should not* take these metaphors as literal messages.

Second, as you begin to explore your dream state, you will recognize that there is absolutely nothing impossible in dreams. If you decide you want something in your dream, you do not work, struggle, or labor long to achieve it. You just intend it and BAM! It's there. Just suppose you could learn how to transition this ability into your day-to-day consensual world–would that be cool or what? The degree to which you become comfortable and proficient in your dream reality is the degree to which you will find your programmed world beginning to collapse.

One of my mentors taught me, "For everything in life, you must pay attention, and to the degree that you do not pay attention, you must pay with pain." If you are spending at least thirty-three percent of your life in an altered state of consciousness, doesn't it stand to reason that there must be some value there beyond just a nap for the conscious mind?

It's similar to the idea of life in other areas of our universe. Our greatest scientists have found thousands upon thousands of universes in just our small span of exploration. In fact, our sun is considered a mediocre star when compared to the suns discovered in other solar systems. Do you think there may be life elsewhere? What is all that space for? Sure seems like wasted space if we are all there is, doesn't it?

The point is that everything has a plan and a purpose, including dream time. Nothing in you or your universe is wasted spiritual energy or mere happenstance. Therefore, the person of power recognizes and constantly explores the full spectrum of possibility.

Begin by placing your journal or a writing pad on your nightstand every night prior to sleep. This step alone sends a strong message to your UCM that you are interested in receiving and remembering your dream time excursions.

Discipline yourself to write your dreams down immediately upon waking–even if it's at 2 AM! It is key to remember that everything in your dream appears as a metaphor. So if you have a dream regarding your best friend, for instance, it is not necessarily about that person, but most likely about what *he or she represents* to you. Always ask, "What does this person, place, or thing represent to me?"

I am often asked to recommend a good book on dreams, to which my answer is, "There are none." If anyone tells you he or she can interpret your dreams for you, walk away! While there are common archetypes and symbols in the collective consciousness, ultimately you must remember they are *your* dreams, and the symbols sent are from *your* unconscious mind. Therefore, you must interpret them yourself through your own filters. While I can teach you a methodology to use for interpretation, I would never consider imposing my interpretation on your dreams–nor, in my experience, should anyone else!

Dreams are there for a reason. Remember, in the life of power, everything counts.

Be Impeccable

BEING impeccable consists of so many different facets. The perennial myth of impeccability tells of the individual in human form who, through commitment, focus, and discipline, elevates himself to the level of the gods.

Through many ages and many cultures we have been taught of these god-men, Dionysus, Osiris, Quetzalcoatl, Wiracocha, Buddha, Christ, and a multitude of others. For each, the myth has been the same: birth, death, transformation, transfiguration, and rebirth.

Unfortunately, when we do not *live out* the messages of the myths, we convert the study "about" them into dogma and create a religion. When this occurs, the role of the great ones immediately becomes oppression versus liberation.

One day, God and Satan are sitting together, drinking some red wine. God produces an envelope. "What do you have there?" asks Satan.

"Truth," answers God.

Satan replies, "How about giving it to me?"

"What will you do with it?" asks God.

Satan replies with a sly smile, "I'll make it into a religion."

The lives and examples of great sages and initiates are to be lived–dogma is to be believed. The former concerns personal experience, impeccability, and the heart–the latter concerns the head. The first calls for massive and continuously impeccable action–the second calls for submission and compliance.

The life of power is a warrior's path, for this great stalker is constantly doing the internal battle with his own demons. Impeccability implies consistently collecting, condensing, and escalating personal energy.

The degree to which you are not impeccable in your life is the degree to which your power will halt–or plummet. In the life of power, everything counts!

Being impeccable is the concept of doing everything to the best of your ability, with the highest intention. It is the process of constantly holding yourself to the utmost standards in every area of your life and, more important, having the willingness to correct yourself when you are not. Being impeccable is a commitment to progressive advancement, growth, and improvement–every moment of every day.

To know about the path is commendable… To walk the path is rare, indeed.

The warrior optimizes energy. Never choose to live at the whim of emotional outbursts, habits of the past, or external circumstances: You must make everything the outcome of your impeccable strategy. Transcending the ego identity of the past, the warrior is free from "need" in the consensual reality. Everyone and everything is recognized as expendable.

Understanding the difference between "choice" and "need," there is no worry or concern for the small and illusionary ego self.

Spirit always desires fuller expression and expansion and, as a spiritual being, expansion is your only objective. Do not fool yourself into thinking that this will be easy. It will not, nor should it be. That is why we call it the path of the misfit, maverick, and outsider, and why it takes a true warrior spirit to pursue that path. By this point you should be well aware that the warrior's path is uncommon. However, it is not elective–it is mandatory. You either get it now... or you will get it later.

A Course in Miracles teaches that every being will eventually reach enlightenment. Since the accession of this expanded state of consciousness is the only reason you manifest in physical form, you might as well commit to the path now. Life gives exams, and if you don't pass... you take them over and over until you do. Once again, there is no option. Again, you either get it now... or you'll get it later.

Let's discuss a few areas of focus for achieving impeccability, beginning with the concept of your word.

In the life of power, your thoughts must be thunder and your word must be law!

The warrior lives by his or her word. This means when you say something will be done, it will be done. When you say you will be somewhere or do something, there is no question: You will be there.

This, like many concepts of the life of power, is not frequently practiced. But then again, you are not the typical tin-soldier, wind-up toy that most people allow themselves to become in life, are you?

Your life is a mirror image of your level of consciousness and power. As your power increases, you rapidly develop the ability to manifest whatever you choose into physical form. Every great tradition has taught that you are "created in the image and likeness" of God Spirit. Therefore, you are a creative being.

As a creator, you must recognize the power you wield, and with great power comes great responsibility. This unbiased power will present you with your own blessings as well as your own curses. You will manifest your hell as quickly as you manifest your heaven. Rocks appear as quickly as diamonds. For this reason, as you continue to reach greater levels in your life, you must be consistently more cognizant of every thought and word.

Quantum physicists tell us that everything in our universe is comprised of the same basic building blocks. The scientist would call this foundation "energy," the theologian would call it "God," and the mystic would call it "Spirit." Ultimately, these terms are only terms–they do not define what they are trying to name. Choose what term works best for you–but focus on and explore the content.

A more important distinction arises in the word *every-thing*. This means that God Spirit resides in all animate and inanimate objects, which obviously includes your thoughts and utterances.

Thoughts are impulses of energy and information, as are words. In the metaphorical book of Genesis, creation of physical entities begins with "And God *said*, 'Let there be light.' "

Your spoken word is a creative, manifesting power.

· What are you speaking into being in your life?

· Are your thoughts and words impeccable?

Every time you speak, you are expending your energy. In the pursuit of power, your focus must be on ensuring that the income and collection of energy always exceeds your expense of energy. You will never collect and condense your energy in the midst of constant expenditure. This does not mean you must become mute–only that you must become more judicious with your word energy.

Be impeccable. If you are not sure you can produce–don't commit to the production. Never say something unless you are certain. If you are constantly making and breaking promises, you lose energy and power. Simplify your communications and only speak when you are certain, centered, and sure.

There are several great teachings that have taught us the importance of guarding the energy of our word. My teacher once told me, "When you have the power... there is nothing to say." This reminds me of the teachings of Lao Tzu, who states, "Those who know do not talk; those who talk do not know." The Gospel of Matthew states, "Let your words be yes, yes, or no, no: for whatever is more than these comes of evil" (delusion). Further, Paul stated, "Use not vain repetitions."

If you are developing your power, you need not clutter your environment and diffuse your energy with meaningless utterances. When you have the power, you don't need to talk about it; you just need to be it.

Another often overlooked area of impeccability is that of thought energy. Every utterance is preceded by a thought.

Many people allow their lower nature to rule their higher nature—and therefore they remain stuck in the life of form.

Thoughts stemming from your lower nature are incongruent with who you say you are or who you are becoming. Thoughts of hatred, jealousy, pride, anger, and fear are thoughts that drain your energy and cause power to decrease. One of the greatest areas of potential power leakages is the area of sexual thoughts.

First, sexual energies are powerful creative energies that are part of the human experience. In many cases, traditional religion has taught that these energies are bad and wrong and should be suppressed. This is ludicrous. No matter how righteous and holy you are, these energies are part of the human experience and do not go away unless severely suppressed—nor should they.

Suppression leads to dysfunction. The sage learns how to experience and harness these energies rather than being harnessed and used by them. This arena may be one of the most challenging battles of impeccability you will ever face. I have had the same challenges you have had—if not more with this one—even before I realized it.

First, let me go on record as saying that I do not believe in the "traditional relationship values" of our historical past. Not all relationships are meant to be for life—in fact, very few are. It was much easier for our ancestors to buy into this life-long partnership philosophy when the average human life span was thirty years and we most likely never left the farm or village. Times have changed, and we must change our viewpoint on relationships as our consciousnesses expand. There are always exceptions, but life is for growth, and when growth has ended, you must either move on or halt your progress. The choice is yours.

Your entire body, every cell and bone, turns over and renews at least every seven years. On a physiological level, that means that your old body dies and is replaced/reborn multiple times during your life journey.

Paul stated, "I die daily" in reference to the spiritual death of ego and the letting go of "childish things." If you are advancing in consciousness, you must let go of the old level of being to allow for the birth of the new. For anything new to live, something old must die.

As a result, if you are dying daily on a physiological and spiritual level, it gives a whole new meaning to " 'til death do us part," doesn't it?

If you are stuck in a rut, living the life of the tin-soldier, wind-up toy like so many other people, then you and your partner died in unison some time ago, and are just waiting for a few more shovels of dirt.

Nothing happens by accident–everything happens for a reason. Some of my greatest teachers in life have been the lovely ladies with whom I have shared my time and my heart. Every couple is brought together to learn from and teach one another. Some lessons take a lifetime, some take years, some take months–and when the lessons are completed, then the relationship has died. I challenge anyone to prove to me that God Spirit wishes you to stay in a non-growing, dead relationship.

While I may have non-traditional relationship viewpoints, I do believe in monogamy, but that was not always the case. There was a period in my life when I thought monogamy was a type of wood.

However, I now know that sexual interaction is a powerful energy exchange, and if you are mixing your energies in a random and varied fashion, you are losing power. You must be impeccable.

During the sexual exchange, the energy field of your partner merges with your energy field and you carry the residual for some time. Sexual union is the ultimate transcendental experience of yang and yin–the active and receptive powers in physical form merging and unifying. Guard your energy field and your creative powers–not only in regard to the physical act, but also in regard to sexual thoughts and imagination.

One of my teachers once asked me, as I blatantly admired a young lady who happened to pass by, "What are your thoughts right now?" I told him, "I was admiring her beauty." Knowing better, he asked me for my specific thoughts, and with much reluctance I admitted they involved more than just admiration. He then informed me that I was performing "sex magic" and that it was leaking energy from my vessel of power.

This was a tough issue for me to tackle, and yet an important part of becoming impeccable. I found as I started keeping inventory of my thoughts in this area that they were not of the highest regard. I am no puritan, nor am I implying that you should be. What I am is a tracker of power, and I assure you that the degree to which your internal world, your words, and your actions do not align, your life is not impeccable and you leak energy and lose power.

Impeccability encompasses all aspects of the life of power. What do you allow yourself to listen to? What do you allow yourself to watch? What do you do with your free time? Is your total life focused on advancement, learning, and enjoyment, or are you allowing your lazy ego to turn your mind into television gelatin?

Who do you spend your time with on a regular basis? Are they fellow warriors committed to meaning and adventure? Or do you have a flock of energy vampires swarming around you?

Are you optimizing your energy? Are you indulging in thoughts of self-importance? Thoughts of worry, doubt, jealousy, hatred, or selfishness? Every thought, every word, every action, every surrounding, and every relationship is either increasing your energy and power or decreasing it–nothing is neutral. If it's not moving you forward, it is holding you back.

Everything counts in the life of power–be impeccable in all areas.

Follow Your Own Passion

PRINCIPLE TWENTY-SIX

I HAVE collected quite a large library over the last 20 years, and I recently happened upon a book I had never read–it discussed the qualities of how to be a CEO. This obviously was not a recent purchase, probably a book I grabbed in some airport during my corporate days. However, I was attracted to it on my library shelf, and I began to flip through it.

The author's suggestion was that you should "always follow the money." While this may be the best route to becoming CEO, I guarantee it is not the route to fulfillment or to power. I spent fifteen years in a large corporation and remember one instance in which I followed this recommended CEO path.

I grew up in the buckle of the Bible belt and started my career in sales. Bound and determined to succeed, I received my first promotion on the anniversary of my second year on the job–I was on my way!

This was quickly followed by multiple promotions, which I actively pursued. I was determined it wouldn't be enough (or so I thought) until I reached the top. I remember an ex-mother-in-law saying to me once, "Son, you always have to follow the money," and I did.

Climbing the ladder of success landed me a big title and a move from Oklahoma to New Jersey! Now, while Jersey has its attractions, it was culture shock for a boy from the Midwest. Moreover, I went from being a big fish in my old job to being a little fish with an empty title and less positional power. I was standing in line with all the other "big titles" waiting my turn at the copy machine. Worse still, my "raise" actually netted me less money due to the massive cost-of-living difference.

I suddenly realized I had invested massive energy and many years achieving something I had been conditioned to want, but that I really didn't want at all. I had bought in and sold out.

The life of power is self-defined, self-referring, and self-sufficient. The warrior refuses to buy in to the collective mindset and all of its trivial pursuits.

While money is necessary for us to operate and grow in today's world, I submit that you will have a more fulfilling life journey if you pursue passion before pay.

Ironically enough, in many–if not most cases–you will have more money if you pursue your passion with excellence and allow the money to come as a by-product. Observe those individuals in your current world who are doing well financially, and you will see that, while there are always exceptions, in most cases this principle holds true.

The warrior realizes that consciousness is the only goal, and if that brings money, toys, and trinkets–so be it. If it doesn't, you are not defined by that, anyway, since that is how the consensual world defines success. You, on the other hand, drive your own bus. The only thing that has any real and lasting value is that which is eternal.

Anything that is not eternal has no real value.

I recently climbed the sacred mountain Salkantay in Peru. This holy pilgrimage to 16,400 feet was the Inca ritual of reuniting with the part of yourself that never left creation–your cosmic double.

While reaching the summit was literally breathtaking, I was once again reminded that the value was in the journey. The days of physical exhaustion, the lack of oxygen, the camping at glacier base, and the hours upon hours of pushing myself to the limit last far longer in memory and have much greater impact than the achievement of the goal.

This principle is true in all areas of life. The majority of your life is spent in "the process" or "the journey" versus "the arriving." Life is way too precious to not be in-joy.

Again, remember you are unique and it is nobler to follow your own passion imperfectly than to perfectly follow someone else's.

Do what you love and love what you do. Follow your own passion before pay–and let the results follow if they do. And if they don't... it really won't matter anyway.

Think Collectively
Principle Twenty-Seven

WHILE the journey of power is individual, the vision must be communal.

One of the greatest things the Inca tradition has taught me is to make decisions based upon the collective and greater good. In the northern hemisphere, we have the North Star as our beacon in the heavens; in the southern hemisphere they have the Southern Cross.

The North Star is alone—an individual—while the Southern Cross is a collection coming together to create something of a higher nature. Do you find your beacon in the North Star or the Southern Cross?

We all come from the same source. These are very exciting times, when spiritual and scientific leaders are once again realizing they are not at odds. In fact, quantum physicists are the mystics of the twenty-first century. Modern science is now making "breakthrough discoveries" that confirm what the mystics have told us since time immemorial. When the scientists finally scale the mountain of truth, they will find the mystics sitting topside, calmly asking, "What took you so long?"

Rupert Sheldrake is a highly awarded and acclaimed biologist as a result of his discovery of "morphogenetic fields." What Sheldrake and others found is that we live in fields of energy and information. What the eyes tell us is empty space is actually a field of power and consciousness.

In his book, *Seven Experiments That Could Change The World*, Sheldrake discusses how a cell can be removed from your body in California, preserved in a petri dish, and flown to New York City. When you get excited in California, the cell in New York vibrates in the petri dish.

This somewhat amazing breakthrough proves that we are connected beyond the physical form and proximity. As mentioned before in this book, current findings also reveal that the myriad of trees in tropical rainforests, once thought to be individual trees, may be growing from one central root system.

These discoveries give new meaning to the concept of "six degrees of separation." This is the idea that all of us are no more than six people away from anyone on the planet. For instance, if you wanted to meet any celebrity, according to this theory, you know someone who knows someone, who knows someone else, and within six people or less you are connected.

The reason to explore six degrees, as well as morphogenetic fields, is to drive home the point that we are all very close and connected. What you do to others you do to yourself.

The warrior understands that anything he does or gives is what he gives to himself.

This is not a new idea, and yet in the light of new insights, you must begin to realize how much power and impact you have on the world at large. Every increment you increase your consciousness and power increases not just yourself but the collective consciousness as well.

All great teachers and sages have understood this *principle* of collective connection. Jesus said, "If I be lifted up, I lift up every man." Unfortunately, historical teachings have propagated the idea that he was speaking only for himself, rather than teaching us a principle by which to live our lives.

Every good thought, word, or deed that you possess for yourself is a gift you give the entire human race. Likewise, every weakening thought, word, or deed you allow to occupy your energy field is a gift (or curse) as well.

Many people want to involve themselves in philanthropic pursuits, yet with a higher awareness, you realize that the greatest philanthropy in which you can involve yourself is self-salvation. The only thing from which you need to be saved is the illusion created by the small ego-self. As a savior of the world, you can only save your self and others by increasing your own consciousness and ending the illusion of separateness.

There are several ways for you to think and make decisions:

Good for self, not good for the community or tribe, and not best for the collective good. This is the approach of the ego on steroids. Thinking only of self is not the way of the sage, and will never bring you to the highest levels of consciousness and power. While you may be able to amass a certain amount of material gain with this approach, your ability will ultimately halt and your joy will be minimized. What you hold back from others will be held from yourself.

Good for self, good for the tribe, not the best for the collective good. This is the cult of patriotism and nationalism–the politicians' dream. Every great empire has eventually fallen as a result of thinking for themselves versus the collective good. We all come from one source, and we live on a round planet–there is no ability to choose sides. There have been more wars and disconnects in history in the name of "God" and property than for any other reasons. War has *nothing* to do with God Spirit! War is a product of the ego god attempting to prove that it is better, wiser, bigger, smarter than, or more loved by the Creator.

Who knows enough to say that their way is the "right way" and that others are "wrong?" We are all one; we all have one objective, whether we are consciously aware of it or not; and all roads originate and end in the same place.

How childish is it to war over an imaginary boundary or property line? How is it that we didn't get over this in our sandbox years? How immature is it to attempt to prove that one prophet is the only prophet—that one teaching is the only teaching? The ego self is the only entity that wants to be "right and better." Your higher self knows that all things are echoes of the one Eternal Source.

Speaking of dividing up the planet, a lot of people want to be concerned for Mother Earth—I, for one, am not concerned. Mother Earth is fine and will be fine long after we stop crawling on her back. If we don't quit squabbling over how to divide her, who owns more of her, and who is most powerful and right, she may get sick of us all and shake us right off into space!

Good for self, good for the tribe, best for the collective. This is the path of power—the way that you as a warrior must walk. When making decisions, if you can discipline yourself to always think collectively, you will find that your decisions, your actions, and your results are more compelling. You will be an initiate of power—you will give the highest to yourself and others—you will be impeccable!

Enlightenment Happens Now

PRINCIPLE TWENTY-EIGHT

THE theory of reincarnation states that you live multiple lives, returning again and again, learning lesson upon lesson, until you "get it right." I consider this to be partially true.

While your higher self is infinite and eternal, your ego self is not. God Spirit is beyond form, actually pre-form. Personalities and individual goals do not exist in this highest realm of consciousness–and this can be corroborated by any other traveler of inner space who has reached this pinnacle of power.

For this reason, I postulate that the traditional ideas regarding reincarnation are the construct of the ego mind attempting to make itself immortal. What you define as yourself (in other words, your ego identity) is not eternal, but *you* are–the *real* you.

Consciousness reincarnates again and again–the person you think yourself to be (your ego/identity) does not. I find it an amusing observation that most individuals who speak of past lives invariably were Cleopatra, Moses, or some other powerful figure. Why wasn't anyone ever shoveling horse manure in Cleopatra's stables or serving falafels to Moses? Someone had to have had those positions, didn't they? Come on!

This sheds an entirely different light upon the ideas of karma and salvation. Karma does not exist for the individual, as there ultimately is no individual–we are all one. The ego identity that thinks itself separate from God Spirit, with its own accomplishments and karma, is self-delusional. Karma is collective, and the objective of consciousness is to consistently experience and advance.

While one individuation of consciousness may be very advanced (individually known as the spiritual warrior, initiate, sage, or adept), the collective consciousness is still quite backward. The current state of world affairs is indicative of the current level collectively achieved.

I recall discussing the idea of collective karma with a person very rooted in the concept of individual karma. She was having a hard time getting her mind around the idea that we did not have to individually pay for our sins. "This absolves everyone of all responsibility for their lives," she commented. Actually, just the opposite is true—you do have to pay. We all have to pay, because we are all one.

The warrior realizes that he/she has the ultimate responsibility of advancing the field of the collective consciousness. For every "sin" (missing the mark), the entire human experience is hindered—for every advancement, the collective pool is increased. Stop and think about this.

> **Not only do you have to pay for your illusion,
> but so does every other manifested being from
> the one collective energy field.**

You should be aware by now that there is only one goal that your higher self has for you, and that goal is enlightenment. You must increase your consciousness and power and escape the low-level energies of the consensual reality. In turn, you advance the consensual reality, and this high objective must happen right now.

The theory that you must reincarnate lifetime after lifetime, trudging along, making mistake after mistake until you finally reach escape velocity, is a bunch of bunk.

The consciousness of the planet is increasing more and more rapidly as each day goes by. The old ideas on reaching enlightenment, like the old ideas on relationships, are not necessarily valid or empowering. We must step into modern timelessness.

When people lived only to the age of thirty, they had to work really hard and fast to make it before they exited their current form–the clock was ticking! However, with longer life expectancy, technological advances, higher levels of education and intelligence, and greater opportunities for life experiences, enlightenment does not have to endure many lives. Besides, if you are not going to reincarnate as the personality you think yourself to be, you had better achieve enlightenment now!

My entire curriculum for the JOURNEY OF POWER, as well as all my tools and learning systems, are designed solely to facilitate this process. There are many tools that technology and increased understanding have afforded us to accelerate this experience.

Most great traditions have their version of the "epiphany/ breakthrough to a higher level of consciousness." Their explanations are weak, as this awakening is something that definitely must be experienced to be understood. You cannot *know* God Spirit–you can only *experience* God Spirit.

In the East they speak of the unleashing of the *Kundalini* energy. This is a sudden rush of power in your etheric body that surges from the lower to the higher chakras. *Satori* is another term for this instantaneous breakthrough in consciousness.

The intellectual, rational mind is the domain of the ego, and while it has its time and place, this is the false identity that must be transcended. Remember, though, that you cannot transcend something you do not have. Remember also that most, if not all, breakthroughs in consciousness are preceded by an ego-death of some nature. My experience is that you have a struggle with reason and eventually reach a rational impasse and/or frustration, at which point you must either break down or break through to a new level of consciousness. This is often facilitated by a loss or some other pain of the physical or ego self. The unfortunate truth is that we rarely do anything to advance unless we experience enough pain in our current situation to get fed up.

This breakthrough is the Kundalini experience–the "blinding light" of Paul on the road to Damascus. The instantaneous leap to a new level of power, understanding, and way of being. And it shatters and rearranges your entire world model. By now, you have at least considered stopping the world. How about shattering your world?

Time is a mental construct. If you go back in history, you realize that time had to be invented. At some point, we just said, "Meet me by the big tree," and we would wait there until someone showed up. I have never seen a lion wearing a watch.

Now is the only time that truly exists–all else is illusion. The past is memory, the future is imagination, and both are illusions of your ego mind. Therefore, there is only one time in which to become enlightened–and that time is now!

Let go of the illusion that enlightenment will come to you in the far-off future or some other lifetime. Make an unbending commitment to be willing to do whatever it takes. This is your shot, warrior. Make it hit the mark.

Live in Flow

PRINCIPLE TWENTY-NINE

A LIFE of power is ultimately living in flow, and in the flow the sage experiences the greatest levels of freedom and power. The ego despises life in flow, desiring instead a life of predictability and control–desiring empty illusions.

Many initially want to walk the path of power because they believe it will give them more control over circumstances. While abilities are developed to manifest and create in a more accomplished fashion, more control over circumstances is not the objective or the outcome. Face it: No matter how badly you desire to control the future, you can't! Therefore, any energy or effort invested in the futile attempt to do so is only setting you up for frustration and failure.

An advancement in consciousness brings you a different *way of experiencing* life. If you call this control, so be it. But the control that true power brings you relates to the *experience* of life, not the situations of life.

Wanting nothing, asking for nothing–allowing, accepting, and embracing everything.

The sage lives a flowing life full of freedom and adventure. Ultimately, the greatest way to gain control is to relinquish control: The greatest level of freedom is a total lack of concern for self. Read the previous sentence again; contemplate it.

Worry and concern for self are rooted in the fear of the finite, identifying with form. When true power is accessed, you *know* the body may be finite and life circumstances may be challenging and difficult, but you are infinite! While the physical body will die–you are eternal! There is a saying in the Zen tradition: "Die before you die, so that when you die, you might live."

Living life in flow is also about letting go of certain needs, rules, and regulations for life's circumstances to be "right" or fulfilling. Think about it: fewer rules, regulations, and needs means infinitely more options. Less is more.

When you surrender to life's ups and downs (a very powerful practice, by the way) instead of attempting to control and avoid ups and downs, you begin to swim with the stream of life energy–not swim against the tide. The Buddha taught, "All of life's suffering is the result of ungratified desire."

While these principles make no sense whatsoever to the ego self, it is the ego alone that feels insecure and threatened. All saving, hoarding, holding on, struggling, being cautious, risk aversion, and insurance come from the ego's uncertainty of what comes next. When much is held, there is much to lose. If nothing is held, there is nothing to lose.

Much can be learned of higher consciousness from babies and animals. I have never seen an animal buying life insurance or a baby worrying about the bills. As previously discussed, the spiritual warrior does not regress to some mythical Eden or baby state of bliss. This so-called blissful state is unconscious incompetence (also known as ignorance).

The warrior moves through ego hell to merge with an *apparently similar* state of true bliss, trust, and flow. However, approaching the starting point once again, you actually arrive for the first time–from a new state of conscious awareness and competence versus unconscious competence and baby-like ignorance. Your hometown has not changed... you have changed.

You don't see, feel, hear, and experience something different in the world: You see, feel, hear, and experience something different in you!

You must go through ego madness to merge with truth.

Security and guarantees based upon illusion are the fodder of the childish ego.

What you and I both know is that no matter what you have, or how much you have, it will never be enough. The ego wants to be reassured and constantly gratified, desiring loads of power and toys. The ego ultimately is nothing more than a big, cumbersome blob of nothing–an image you have created for yourself out of imagination and memory that will ultimately die. You did not come in with it, and you will not leave with it.

As you embrace the infinite, you begin to live in flow. You transcend the ego and all of its little games and inadequacies and operate from a higher order. Life in flow asks for no physical guarantees, because you ultimately realize there are none. I have known countless multi-millionaires who thought life was set and secure, only to lose it all in one stock market dip.

True power is recognition that security and guarantees can only reside within. Like traveling in a heavy fog in which you can only see a few steps ahead of you, when you are in the flow, you focus entirely on the task and experience at hand. Everything becomes beautifully spontaneous and perfect.

The need to "feel secure" is only a socialized belief system–a bad habit that has been developed and passed down through history. Where did it originate in our collective consciousness? Babies don't enter with this "I must be secure" mentality, and certainly primal man did not possess it. Children don't concern themselves with anything–when they are hungry, they cry and food arrives. Everything they need is given to them.

The warrior recognizes that his security comes from a state of consciousness, and that all else is transitory and fleeting. The small ego wants to know everything that will happen next, but your infinite self already knows.

Letting go of the ego and living in flow, you will feel the need to impress, convince, or "be right" diminish. Only insecure and imaginary entities can be threatened–that which is real is eternal. There is no need to prove anything any longer: When you have the power, there is nothing necessary to say. Those who speak do not know, and those who know do not speak.

Struggle becomes a practice of the distant past as you realize that it was never necessary: Life was never meant to be a struggle. Life is an eternal dance, a glorious game to be played to the fullest. When living in flow, there is no struggle–only play.

Hurry is fear disguised as passion.

There is no need to slow down, only to calm down. With power, you realize there is no need to hurry. Every great teacher and saint has told us that we should never worry, toil, or attempt to predict tomorrow. The spiritual warrior sees those who hurry and worry and discerns that "hurry is fear disguised as passion." "I *really am* passionate!" you may say. Maybe. Be cautious–make sure you are not fueled by doubt or fear. When you truly *know*, you never struggle, worry, or hurry. When you know, you just move forward in power, experiencing the present moment in all its glory and letting the future take care of itself.

As you move into the realm of the spiritual warrior, there is less and less planning. You find instead an elegant way of operating intuitively. When faced with a decision, ask consistently, "Does this feel right?" "Does this feel like a decision and/or action I should move upon?"

Analysis is the product of the ego. Refusing the seduction of analysis, you act upon those intuitive messages that often make no sense whatsoever to the intellectual ego, but are *always* right. There is a time for calm, centered, yet massive action–and there is a time to wait. The discipline to wait is just as powerful as taking massive action.

You recognize that the ego is the only part of you that will never be wealthy. No matter what you save or possess, it will never be enough. It must always be bigger, better, faster, more. Yet the sage recognizes that all that is really needed is joy and peace–a sense of certainty and calm irrespective of life circumstances.

Routine becomes death. Spontaneity, quest, risk, and exploration are the fruits from which the juice of life is squeezed. Perfection is not defined as a certain outcome, but rather a state of *living and being*. You release that which your ego has told you the world "should be," and you begin to constantly celebrate what life is. All things are recognized as perfect and exciting, just the way they are.

Arriving at a point of not knowing the particulars of the future, and being totally secure with this place, you are truly wealthy and free. You can finally say with certainty that you are self-sufficient.

You move from "believing" to *knowing*. You know you are a spiritual being. You are not your body, your emotions, your personality, or your ego. You are a magnificent spiritual power, a unique thumbprint of the infinite. You are divine energy evolving upward through the complexities of body, emotions, and mind to comprehend yourself as an unstoppable, abundant spiritual power, eternally growing and expanding. You are grounded in infinity yet happily experiencing "human being."

The life of power is *the quickening*–the escalation of power, the opening of spiritual awareness and true wealth. Living in flow is the ultimate in joy and knowing: a heroic quest so completely anchored in your own infinite self that you have no need whatsoever to predict and control. Each and every day is a glorious gift, sacred play, and each life experience an amazing adventure and opportunity.

About James Arthur Ray

As a self-made millionaire and business owner, James is one of few spiritual teachers who has achieved top honors in the business world and has thrived as an entrepreneur for over 15 years. His background in behavioral sciences and entrepreneurship, coupled with his avid spiritual quest, gives him a unique and powerful ability to address life issues from an integrated and comprehensive level.

Recently recognized in the *San Diego Business Journal* as one of the fastest-growing entrepreneurial businesses in the area, James Ray International is a multi-million dollar business specializing in teaching individuals how to create wealth in all areas of their life: financial, relational, intellectual, physical, and spiritual.

Prior to his entrepreneurial success, James had a flourishing corporate career, during which he spent over five years as one of AT&T's top sales managers, four years as a personal and business growth expert with AT&T School of Business, and four years working with best-selling author Stephen Covey.

James has studied and been exposed to a wide diversity of teachings and teachers: from traditional college and the business schools of AT&T to the ancient cultures of Peru and Egypt and the jungles of the Amazon. As a result, he has the unique ability to blend the mystical and practical into a usable and easy-to-access formula.

Because of his comprehensive background, James considers himself a "practical mystic." His JOURNEY OF POWER curriculum is the fusion of wealth-building principles and success strategies, as well as the teachings of all great spiritual traditions, mystery schools, and esoteric studies that James has experienced and assimilated over the last twenty-five years.

When he is not on retreat learning from his spiritual mentors, James conducts more than 150 days of public appearances and seminars each year. As a coach and teacher, James has helped hundreds of individuals and organizations create harmony and wealth in all areas of their business and life.

About the Journey of Power®

FOLLOW this easy roadmap to create an abundant, wealthy and fulfilled life...

Embark on your JOURNEY OF POWER. Do you have a dream or goal that you've longed to achieve but haven't yet? In this powerful life-changing experience, you embark upon a journey of increasing power and accomplishment, blending the latest and greatest findings in science, philosophy, psychology, business strategy, and just good common sense.

You'll learn to quickly and easily increase your wealth in all areas of your life–financial, relational, intellectual, physical, and spiritual. When you've achieved this result, you are really wealthy–you possess true Harmonic Wealth®.

We live in a time in history unlike any before it–a time when the greatest scientific breakthroughs prove you have the ability to literally create anything and everything you desire.

No matter how successful you are, deep down inside, you know there's more to life...

Your gut instincts tell you life is not really meant to be a struggle, yet you've been brainwashed to think that only sweat and hard work will get you where you want to be. Here's a better way...

Let the Journey of Power be your roadmap to an abundant, wealthy and fulfilled life.

You have to learn to walk before you can run...
to run before you fly.

Harmonic Wealth is not acquired in one book, one experience or one event—it's earned through concentrated energy and focus. The JOURNEY OF POWER is not a "get rich quick" program, nor will it make you lose weight over night... grow thicker hair... or have an instantly brighter smile.

It's far more powerful and achievable than that.

The JOURNEY OF POWER bridges the most powerful concepts from the nuts-and-bolts world of success and the spiritual world of true happiness. Achieving outrageous results takes work! If it happened over night, everyone would do it.

But it's not as hard as you think, and the process is incredibly fun and satisfying.

Regardless of your current understanding, education, or skill, if you're willing to roll up your sleeves and get to work, it will put you into high gear like nothing you have ever experienced.

Simply put... it will change your life.

FOR MORE INFORMATION ON PRODUCTS AND
EVENTS BY JAMES RAY, VISIT WWW.JAMESRAY.COM